M SAIC
Techniques & Traditions
Projects & Designs from Around the World

SONIA KING

STERLING PUBLISHING CO., INC.
NEW YORK

Front Cover: **Sonia King.** *Pacific Rim*, 2002. 11 x 14 x 14 inches (28 x 35 x 35 cm). Glass, ceramic, paua shell.

Page 2: **Felice Nittolo.** *Light* (detail of the installation), 1999. Marble, smalti, and gold. Photo by the artist.

Photo Credits:

Chapter 2: All photos by Sheila Cunningham except where otherwise noted.

Chapter 3: All photos by Sheila Cunningham except 3–32 by author and where otherwise noted.

Chapter 5: All photos by Sheila Cunningham except finished house number project (page 111), 5–2 to 5–7, and 5–18 to 5–21 by author.

Chapter 6: Project and instruction photos by author except for 6–7, 6–13 to 6–24 by Sheila Cunningham.

Chapter 7: Project and instruction photos by author except for finished sun project (page 168), 7–10, 7–13, finished mood totem project (page 174), 7–22 to 7–24 by Sheila Cunningham.

Chapter 8: Project and instruction photos by author except for 8–3, 8–8, 8–16, 8–21 by Sheila Cunningham.

EDITED BY HAZEL CHAN
DESIGN BY 27.12 DESIGN LTD.

Library of Congress Cataloging-in-Publication Data

King, Sonia.
 Mosaic techniques & traditions : projects & designs from around the world / Sonia King.
 p. cm.
Includes index.
 ISBN 0-8069-7577-6
1. Mosaics. 2. Mosaics–Technique. I. Title: Mosaics techniques & traditions. II. Title.
 NA3750 .K56 2002
 738.5–dc21

                                                             2002008494

10 9 8 7 6 5 4 3

Published by Sterling Publishing Co., Inc.
387 Park Avenue South, New York, NY 10016
© 2003 by Sonia King
Distributed in Canada by Sterling Publishing
c/o Canadian Manda Group, 165 Dufferin Street
Toronto, Ontario, Canada M6K 3H6
Distributed in Great Britain by Chrysalis Books Group PLC
The Chrysalis Building, Bramley Road, London W10 6SP, England
Distributed in Australia by Capricorn Link (Australia) Pty. Ltd.
P.O. Box 704, Windsor, NSW 2756, Australia

Printed in China
All rights reserved

Sterling ISBN 0-8069-7577-6

SAFETY NOTICE
Making mosaics can be dangerous. Readers should follow the safety procedures mentioned in this book. Wear safety glasses and protective clothes during the preparing of the tesserae and creating of the mosaics. Neither the author, copyright holders, nor publishers of this book can accept legal liability for any damage or injury sustained as a result of making mosaics.

CONTENTS

ACKNOWLEDGMENTS

This book wouldn't be complete without the generous contribution of mosaic artists around the world. More than two hundred artists submitted over 1600 images of truly fabulous work. I am inspired and humbled. I only wish there were room for every image. Writing a book on the world of mosaics is destined to be incomplete in some way. Any omissions or errors are my own.

I would like to pay homage to Emma Biggs, Elaine M. Goodwin, and Jane Muir for their talent, generous guidance, and friendship. I owe much of what I know as well as my aspirations in mosaics to them. For their support and encouragement, many thanks go to my dear friend and talented mosaicist George Fishman and his wife, Nancy Ancrum, my partner in gelato crimes.

Special thanks to Carmen Ramirez and Debbie Ernst, two of my students who kindly volunteered to help manage the slide submissions and database. I would still be typing without them. Thanks to Sheila Cunningham for her creativity, unfailing support, good humor,

Sonia King. *Path,* 2001. Ceramic, glass, marble, shell, gold. 9 inches x 11 feet 4 inches (23 cm x 3.5 m). Photo by author.

 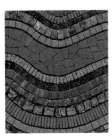    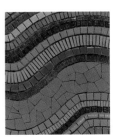

and great photography. Leigh Davis' assistance in the studio made it possible to keep projects moving along.

Thanks is owed to Phil Ober of Expert Imaging for helping me over many of the photography hurdles. Diana Thatcher of Splendor in the Grass generously assisted with the statuary. Anna Finelli of Ravennarte translated the call to artists into Italian, thereby extending the reach of this book. Liz Wagner, instructor in metal sculpture at the Creative Arts Center of Dallas, kindly created the great table base for the indirect project in Chapter 5. Sandy Robertson, fellow mosaic artist, provided the original concept for the sun disks in Chapter 8. Jean Ann Dabb, Associate Professor of Art History at Mary Washington College, reviewed the "History" chapter. Danielle Truscott and Hazel Chan at Sterling Publishing and Jen Harte at 27.12 Design Ltd. made this whole venture possible as well as a pleasure.

Vince Hall has helped me achieve so many things. He is a friend and a mentor whose confidence, support, and guidance mean a great deal. My pal Pete Peterson has watched me pull lots of rabbits out of hats and still believes in me.

No one could have a stronger supporter or better friend than Joan Martin. Teri Wells patiently put up with my absence from our long-standing friendship. To my dear friend Bonny Urschel, thank you for dragging me out of the studio for our walks and listening to me whimper about deadlines. And thanks also to my many students who never fail to teach me. And I have to express my admiration for my brother, Jerry King, who gave me the ability to take a joke and is a champion at showing true grace under impossible circumstances.

Finally, I would like to thank my parents whose very different contributions have made this book possible. My dad, Warner King, instilled a love of travel and the desire to explore new places. He certainly qualifies as my "patron of the arts." And my mom, Sherri King, who made her first mosaics in the 1960s and is still creating great mosaic art today. Inheriting a small bit of her style, color sense, and passion would make anyone a star. I couldn't have done this without her.

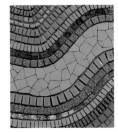   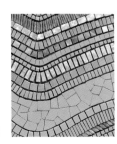  

INTRODUCTION

Opposite Page: **Theatrical Mask of an Old Woman**, third century C.E. Museo d'Arqueologia, Barcelona, Spain. Photo by author.

Above: **Cleo Mussi.** *Platter Faces*, 2001. 9 x 6 inches (22 x 16 cm) and 19 x 14 inches (48 x 35 cm). Recycled china. Photo by the artist.

The art of mosaic appeals to a broad range of tastes. Many see it as a fine-art medium, like sculpture, assemblage, or painting. Others view it as a craft, decorative art, or architectural treatment. This book looks at mosaics from all the angles, showing many genre and variations of the art as well as the techniques in making your own mosaics.

The process of creating a mosaic is captivating on many levels. The materials themselves are fascinating: the colors, textures, and reflective qualities. Even finding materials is an absorbing job: Italian smalti, recycled china, ceramic, and glass tiles. Nipping pieces and fitting them together to create something is both relaxing and mentally stimulating. It's easy to get lost in the process for hours.

In a successful mosaic, the materials, the way they are laid, and the image must all work together. Each individual piece, or tessera, retains its individual identity yet the eye assimilates the pieces into a whole image. There is an interdependence between what is defined by the tesserae and what's implied. This is very different from a painting or drawing, where the medium is subservient to the image. When you view the historical and contemporary mosaics in this book, you will be inspired and energized by the balance of material and image. Over a hundred artists from around the globe have generously contributed images of their work to this book. The quality of the work is a testament to their talent and the current popularity of mosaics.

Top: **The Nile Mosaic** (detail), first century B.C.E. Museo Nazionale Archeologico Prenestino, Palestrina, Italy. Photo by author.

Center: **Partridge**, fourth century C.E. Basilica of Aquileia, Italy. Photo by author.

Bottom: **Child on a Tiger**, House of the Faun, Pompeii, second century B.C.E. Nat'l Archeological Museum, Naples, Italy. Photo by author.

Opposite Page: **Black and White Floor**, first century C.E. Archeological Complex. Russi, Italy. Photo by author.

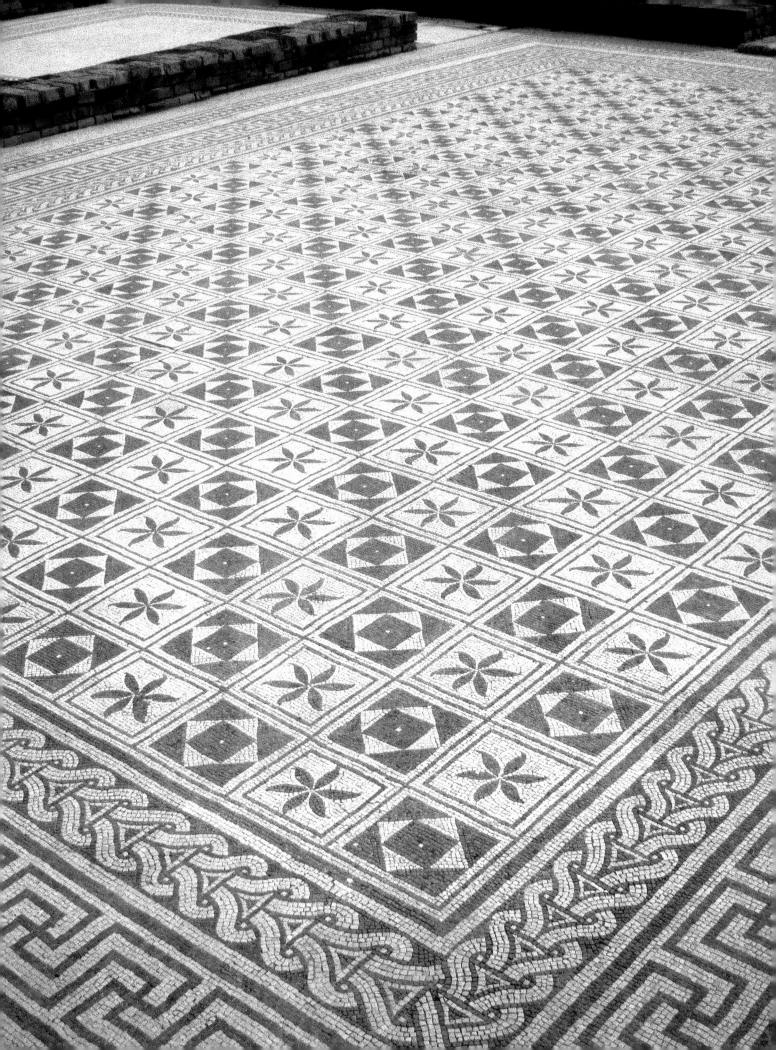

This book is arranged geographically with a stimulating array of visuals throughout. First, there is a brief history of mosaics. Instructional information follows in four large chapters. "Materials and Tools" includes detailed descriptions of materials, tools, bases, adhesives, and more. The "Techniques" chapter covers the skills you need to create mosaics, from shaping the tesserae to preparing the base to mixing grout. "Designing a Mosaic" offers both practical and aesthetic instructions, plus a design checklist, for creating your own mosaic. The "Creating a Mosaic" chapter brings everything together with the two primary methods in creating a mosaic: direct and indirect. Included is a project for each method given in detailed, step-by-step instructions.

The next three chapters span the world: "Europe," "The Americas," and "Around the Globe." Each region includes five projects of varying difficulty: easy, intermediate and advanced. The projects derive from historical, contemporary, and geographical inspirations. The galleries throughout these three chapters include the works of contem-

Opposite Page: **Antoni Gaudí** and **Josep M. Jujol.** Undulating Bench, 1905–1914. Ceramic and glass. Park Güell, Barcelona, Spain. Photo by author.

Above: **Neonian Baptistry**, fifth century C.E. Ravenna, Italy. Photo by author.

porary artists as well as works in the local traditions. Each region also has recommended mosaic sites to see.

Some readers may only want to make a platter or a vase. This book will help them do that, but I hope it will also give them an appreciation for the skill, talent, and passion of those who pursue mosaics as a fine-art medium. Others may be looking for technical information to increase their proficiency. I've tried to "tell all" so those with some experience may learn something new. Some readers may be interested in the eye-candy: stunning visuals of a great variety of works, both historical and contemporary, and a guide to visiting mosaics around the world. While the "Sites to See" lists are not exhaustive, they are wonderful introductions to discovering different mosaics and mosaicists around the world.

Les Moutons (detail), 1896. Institut Pasteur, Paris. © Institut Pasteur.

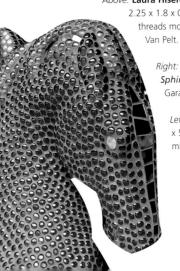

Above: **Laura Hiserote.** *Rite of Passage*, 2000.
2.25 x 1.8 x 0.2 inches (57 x 46 x 4 mm). 16,394 glass threads mounted in 22k gold. Photo by Erica and Harold Van Pelt.

Right: **Niki de Saint Phalle.** *The Empress (The Sphinx)*, 1978–1990. Il Gardena dei Tarocchi, near Garavicchio, Italy. Photo by author.

Left: **Sonia King.** *Flying Colors* (detail), 2001. 6.8 x 5 x 31.5 feet (2.1 x 1.5 x 9.6 m). Marble gems, mirror. Photo by Sheila Cunningham.

Matthias Biehler, realized by School of Mosaics under direction of **Luciana Notturni. Mosaic Coat and Bench,** 2000. Smalti. Ravenna, Italy. Photo by author.

Lillian Sizemore and **Laurel True.** *Mission Creek Mural* (detail), 1999. Ceramic and mirror. San Francisco, CA. Photo by Laurel True.

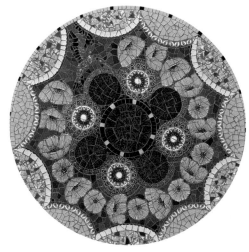

Above: **Maggy Howarth.** *Compass & Winds* (detail), 1992. Pebbles. Photo by Spanfoto.

Right: **Valerie Carmet.** *Colibri,* 2001. 42-inch (1.1-m) diameter. Dishes. Photo by Preston-Schlebusch.

What I hope all my readers will take from this book is that creating a mosaic offers a unique opportunity for individual expression. I believe that you could put ten people in a room, give each the same materials and tools, give each the same design to create, and no two mosaics would come out remotely alike. On that note, I encourage you to use the projects in the book as a starting point for your own creations. Switch the colors, change the materials, alter the design, feel free to take a chance. The art of mosaics is not only liberating, but it is also very forgiving and its lessons can extend far beyond the tesserae and design. I often say to my students that the most valuable lesson I can teach them is how to solve the problem of the difficult piece. When working a mosaic, you'll often find a spot that needs an odd-shaped tessera that's difficult to cut. Invariably, that piece isn't the problem. Look back three or four tesserae and you'll usually find a piece that's slightly off. That anomaly can ripple through a mosaic and result in the need for the problem piece. If you fix the odd piece back at the start, the problem solves itself. After the umpteenth time I said that in class, a student responded, "Ooh, that's just like life." And she's right.

Previous Pages: **Marco Bravura.** *Floating Carpet*, 1997. 16.5 x 11.5 feet (5 x 3.5 m). Smalti. Cervia, Italy. Photo by Maurizio Montanari.

Right: **Candace Bahouth.** *Mosaic Chair No. 2*, 2000. 54 x 31 x 32 inches (137 x 79 x 81 cm). Unglazed ceramic and golds. Photo by artist.

Opposite Page: **Lucio Orsoni.** *Black and Copper Gold*, 1972. 36 x 36 inches (89 x 89 cm). Smalti and gold. Photo by artist.

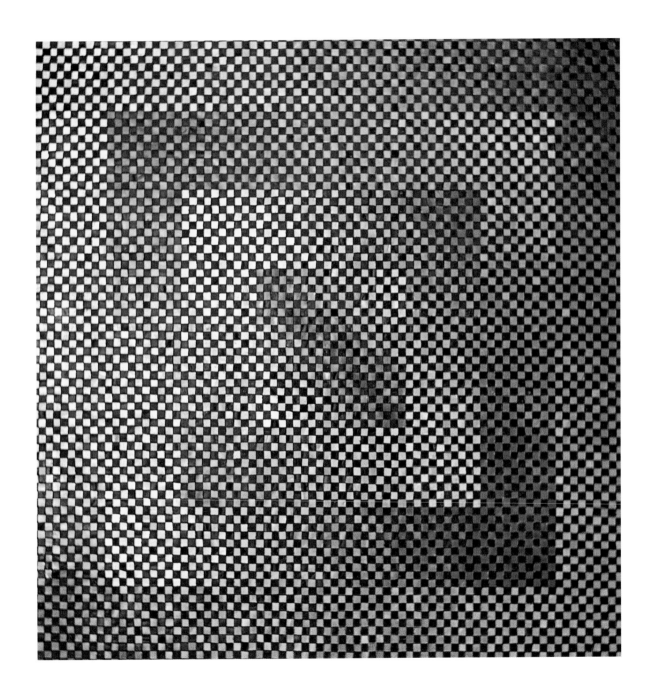

HISTORY

The art of mosaics has a long history stretching back 5000 years. Despite many upswings and downturns in popularity, its appeal has endured. Studying these ancient mosaics offers a valuable connection to the traditions of mosaic art. Many mosaicists of the past were absolute masters. Not only are many of the techniques and materials used then essentially the same today, but there is also a wealth of ideas and inspiration to be found in their work. For instance, the Romans usually worked with a limited palette of colors, yet they were able to create mosaics of incredible expressiveness with stones in a few shades. Look at the two guardsmen in the second century mosaic from the Bardo Museum in Tunis (Photo 1–2). The work has a freshness and boldness that is apparent even today. The eye is created from only fifteen tesserae (Photo 1–3). It's interesting that the guardsmen in the mosaics

1–1 Opposite Page: **Portrait of an Athlete**, third century C.E. Archeological Museum, Aquileia, Italy. Photo by author.

1–2 Top: **Two Guardsmen**, second century C.E. Bardo Museum, Tunis, Tunisia. Photo by author.

1–3 Left: **Two Guardsmen** (detail), second century C.E. Bardo Museum, Tunis, Tunisia. Photo by author.

1–4 Top: **Neptune in Triumph**, late second century C.E. Bardo Museum, Tunis, Tunisia. Photo by author.

1–5 Bottom Left: **The Baptism**, fifth century C.E. Arian Baptistry, Ravenna, Italy. Photo by author.

1–6 Center Right: **Medieval Warrior**, thirteenth century C.E. San Giovanni, Ravenna, Italy. Photo by author.

1–7 Bottom Right: **Guardsmen**, seventh century C.E. Palazzo di Teodorico, Ravenna, Italy. Photo by author.

from the seventh and thirteenth centuries display a lesser-skill level (Photos 1–6 and 1–7). (Progress doesn't always move in a straight line.)

Mosaicists from the Byzantine era teach us about working with light. For example, when working on vaults in Byzantine churches, they pushed gold tesserae into the mortar at different angles to achieve maximum light reflection. My favorite lesson to look for is different treatments of water and transparency created from opaque tesserae (Photos 1–4 and 1–5).

One reason why we have so many fine examples of historic mosaics to study and learn from is the durability of the materials. Pebbles, marble, and glass create enduring works of art that, unlike frescoes, are relatively impervious to water damage. Another reason for the abundance of historic mosaics is that most of the early mosaics were floors and pavements. When the buildings collapsed, the floors were buried and protected until later excavations uncovered them. When mosaics moved up onto walls and ceilings in later years, they were often in churches that remained in use and were maintained for a very long time.

New mosaics are still being discovered today. Zeugma, in southeastern Turkey, was founded in 300 B.C.E. as a Hellenist city that saw great prosperity during Roman times because of its location on the trade route to the East. The prosperity of the city was reflected in fabulous mosaics that decorated the homes. Recently, beautiful polychrome mosaics were found in Zeugma, but a dam for a hydroelectric project had flooded two-thirds of the area of this rich site. Heroic efforts were made to save as much as possible before the flooding, but it is certain that many mosaics await excavation by future generations.

The earliest examples of mosaic art are commonly agreed to be Sumerian. Around 3000 B.C.E.

1–8 Top: **Pebble Mosaic Path**, fifteenth century c.e. Topkapi Palace, Istanbul, Turkey. Photo by author.

1–9 Center: **Archeological Site**, fourth century c.e. Seviac, France. Photo by author.

1–10 Bottom: **Grape Leaf Emblema**, fourth century c.e. Archeological Site, Seviac, France. Photo by author.

in Mesopotamia, clay cones were pushed point-first into mud walls and columns. The different-colored bottoms of the cones created various patterns. While the cones weren't flat like Roman tesserae, the resulting surface was a creation made from fitting together many small pieces to create a whole. Approximately 400 years later, around 2600 B.C.E., mosaics were used in the kingdom of Ur, part of modern Iraq, to decorate vessels and small objects. The "Standard of Ur," which can be seen at the British Museum, is a wooden box decorated with pieces of shell, lapis lazuli, and limestone depicting the figures of men and animals.

By 600 B.C.E., the Greeks were creating floor mosaics. Early pebble mosaics, discovered at Delphi, were made of black and white water-smoothed stones used to create geometric patterns in the pavements. Soon after, figural mosaics appeared that were also created from black and white pebbles set into a brown mortar. Some fine examples exist from Olynthus circa 400 B.C.E. This development was followed by the introduction of color around 300 B.C.E. In Pella, strips of lead, and sometimes clay, were used to outline some forms that were created from finer pebbles in a range of tones to offer more detail. Over the next hundred years, the water-smoothed pebbles evolved to cut pieces of stone that ultimately obtained the regularity of cubed tesserae. Around 150 B.C.E., mosaics from Delos, a rich trading city, utilized a broader palette of colors as tesserae of colored glass began to be used. No longer reserved for the elite, the art was accepted and available to middle-class merchants and officials. Mosaics were being used in many rooms of houses.

During the classical period of Greek history (approximately 450 B.C.E. to 350 B.C.E.), artists pursued the ideal in the human form. This was a change from the earlier focus on geometric and

1–11 Opposite Page: **Nile Mosaic**, first century B.C.E. Museo Nazionale Archeologico Prenestino, Palestrina, Italy. Photo by author.

1–12 Top: **Nile Mosaic** (detail), first century B.C.E. Museo Nazionale Archeologico Prenestino, Palestrina, Italy. Photo by author.

1–13 Bottom: **Venus**, fourth century C.E. Musée de Carthage, Tunisia. Photo by author.

Naples and dated to the second century B.C.E. Known as the Alexander Mosaic (Photo 1–19), it depicts the Battle of Issus between Alexander and the Persian King Darius. Although the palette is limited to black, white, red, brown, and yellow, it is a naturalistic and convincing depiction with finely executed shading and detail. The tesserae are tiny, maybe ⅛ inch (3 mm) square, and there are estimated to be well over a million pieces used in the mosaic.

Around the first century B.C.E., black and white floor mosaics became very popular in the Roman world. Because of their repetitive designs, they were more economical to create than figurative mosaics, yet they still offered the same practical considerations, such as durability. Notice how the floor in Russi, Italy has survived despite the sinking of the earth below it (Photo 1–20). The Romans created floor mosaics in geometric patterns (Photos 1–21 and 1–22) that predate Op Art by several thousand

1–19 Top: **Alexander from** *The Battle of Issus,* **Pompeii** (detail), second century B.C.E. 8 x 15 feet (2.4 x 4.6 m). Nat'l Archeological Museum, Naples, Italy. Photo by author.

years. Figures were represented in silhouette and the coursing, or *andamento,* of the tesserae defined both movement and form (Photo 1–25). Ostia, outside Rome, and Russi, near Ravenna, have some wonderful black and white mosaics. Another variation for floors was *Opus signinum,* which featured tesserae laid in geometric designs with a mortar of crushed terra-cotta (Photo 1–23).

Pompeii and Herculaneum were wealthy cities where mosaics were a popular display of a homeowner's wealth. Their destruction by the eruption of Mount Vesuvius in 79 C.E. offers firm dating for many of the mosaics in the region. In Pompeii, several threshold mosaics were found to serve a functional purpose. They showed a dog straining at its leash with the Latin words: *Cave Canem,* or "Beware of Dog." By this time, colored glass tesserae were in common usage and the Romans installed mosaics on walls as well as floors. Wall mosaics (Photo 1–29) had several advantages over frescoes as the colors were much brighter and would last in the hot, damp air of the baths.

Further afield in the Roman Empire, North

Africa has a wealth of ancient mosaics. Carthage was another center for mosaicists of great skill. The Bardo Museum (Photo 1–31) in Tunis has probably the largest mosaics collection in the world. It offers a unique opportunity to study a variety of styles in one place. The walls of this old palace are covered from floor to ceiling with fabulous mosaics. It is a good reminder of the prevalence of the art form in ancient times. The collection includes wonderful figurative and animal mosaics as well as some with mythological subjects (Photo 1–33). The examples of emblemata are among the finest, showing great detail and skill. Note the quality of the image and the small tesserae in the emblema of Spring (Photo 1–34) compared to the larger tesserae and coarser laying in the background. It's easy to see the difference between the work of a master and an apprentice.

Many mosaics from North Africa feature animals and natural scenes on a neutral background. Piazza Amerina, nearby in central Sicily, is perhaps

1–20 Above Left: **Black and white floor showing effects of subsidence over time,** first century c.e. Archeological Complex, Russi, Italy. Photo by author.

1–21 Left: ***Head of Medusa,*** second century c.e. National Roman Museum, Rome. Photo by author.

1–22 Bottom Right: **Geometric Floor Mosaic,** first to second century c.e. Museo d'Arqueologia, Barcelona, Spain. Photo by author.

1–23 *Top Left:* **Opus signinum** (mortar with terra-cotta aggregate), first century C.E. Ampurias, Spain. Photo by Dugald MacInnes.

1–24 *Above:* **Birds and Trees**, fourth century C.E. Museo d'Arqueologia, Barcelona, Spain. Photo by author.

1–25 *Top Right:* **Bath of the Cart Drivers**, second century C.E. Ostia Antica, Rome. Photo by author.

1–26 *Opposite Page, Top:* **Two Comedy Masks**, second century C.E. National Roman Museum, Rome. Photo by author.

the most impressive example of this style. The site is thought to have been a villa for the Roman governor, Maximianus Herculius, who died in 310 C.E. There are over 35,000 square feet (3150 sq m) of magnificent mosaic floors. The Great Hunt mosaic (Photo 1–39) covers a corridor over 200 feet (61 m) long and features all sorts of exotic animals in a variety of scenes. Other rooms include the labors of Hercules, girls exercising in bikinis (Photo 1–40), and various animals from ducks to elephants.

The mosaics in the Great Palace in Istanbul, then known as Constantinople, are from a later date

but show a similarity of style. Although these mosaics can't compete in quantity with those in Piazza Amerina, they also are of great interest. The range of subject matter in a relatively small area includes a monkey wearing a robe and gathering dates as well as two leopards eating a deer (Photo 1–41). They are all displayed in vignettes on a neutral background. The relaxed and natural forms of the animals show the great skill of the artist(s).

By the fourth century C.E., Christianity was spreading through the failing Roman Empire and the imagery of mosaics began to change. The basilica

1-27 Bow mosaic from the time of Augustus, first century C.E. Archeological Museum, Aquileia, Italy. Photo by author.

1-28 Flower Bouquet, second century C.E. National Roman Museum, Rome. Photo by author.

1–29 *Opposite Page:* **Neptune and Amphitrite**, second century B.C.E. Herculaneum, Italy. Photo by author.

1–30 *Top Left:* **Dionysus as a Child**, third century C.E. Bardo Museum, Tunis, Tunisia. Photo by author.

1–31 *Top Right:* A small section of the huge collection of Roman mosaics at the Bardo Museum. Tunis, Tunisia. Photo by author.

1–32 *Center:* **The Boar Hunt,** third to the fourth century C.E. Piazza Amerina, Sicily, Italy. Photo by author.

1–33 *Below Left:* **Adornment of Venus** (possibly a reproduction). Carthage, Tunisia. Photo by author.

1-34 *Spring Emblema of the Four Seasons*, third century c.e. Bardo Museum, Tunis, Tunisia. Photo by author.

at Aquileia has an interesting mix of Roman and early Christian subjects. There are depictions of birds (Photo 1–44) and other animals. In one mosaic, a fight between a rooster and a turtle (Photo 1–42) symbolizes the early struggles of the religion. In a different area, the floor is a pattern of borders mixed with lettering and symbolic imagery (Photo 1–45).

During the third century, the Roman Empire experienced further upheaval and ultimately split into an Eastern and Western Empire. Early in the fourth century, Constantine reunited the empire and moved the capital to Byzantium (later called Constantinople and today known as Istanbul). Constantine declared Christianity the official religion of the empire and that prompted a whole new purpose and style of mosaic art. Roman mosaics had been primarily private commissions that reflected the wealth of the patron. With the transition to the Christian era, Byzantine mosaics were created for the church, emperors, and governmental authorities. The unification of church and state

led to increased budgets. The goal of the mosaics was to induce awe in the worshippers. As a result, there were few limitations on size, and expensive materials, like gold sandwiched between two layers of glass, became common. The color palette of glass smalti also increased.

Walls and vaults offered the perfect surfaces for using golds to present the religion in the best light.

The enhanced colors and reflectivity of the golds and glass made the wall and ceiling mosaics objects of wonder. The Romans presented the natural world and mythological subjects in an idealized image. Later mosaics showed Christendom in a stylized manner by codifying the religion for the faithful. Skilled mosaic artists overcame the design problem of foreshortening that was created by raising the mosaics above the eye level of the viewer. They even took into account where the viewers would be standing by pushing the tesserae into the mortar at angles that would achieve the maximum light reflection.

After Constantine's death in 337, the empire split again into the Western and Eastern Empire. Ravenna, a wealthy port city south of Venice, became the capital of the Western Empire. There, rich patrons sponsored mosaic art in churches as a visible display of their piety. The quality and quantity of Ravenna's Byzantine era mosaics earned it a UNESCO designation as a World Heritage Site. A Latin inscription on the wall of the Archepisco-

1–35 Opposite Page, Bottom: **Neriad with Dolphins,** third to fourth century C.E. Piazza Amerina, Sicily, Italy. Photo by author.

1–36 Above: **The Three Graces** (detail), third to fourth century C.E. Museo d'Arqueologia, Barcelona, Spain. Photo by author.

1–37 Top Right: **Venus,** second century C.E. Bardo Museum, Tunis, Tunisia. Photo by author.

1–38 Bottom Right: **Dionysus Watering the Flowers,** second century C.E. Vatican Museum, Rome. Photo by author.

1–39 *Top:* **The Great Hunt, Loading of the Ostrich**, third to fourth century C.E. Piazza Amerina, Sicily, Italy. Photo by author.

1–40 *Center:* **Girls Exercising in Bikinis**, third to fourth century C.E. Piazza Amerina, Sicily, Italy. Photo by author.

1–41 *Bottom:* **Leopards with a Deer**, fourth century C.E. The Great Palace, Istanbul, Turkey. Photo by author.

palian Chapel describes the mosaics as *Aut Lux hic nata est aut capta hic libera regnat*, which translates to "Either light was born here or, captured here, reigns freely." The Mausoleum of Galla Placida in Ravenna was created in the fifth century C.E. The dome is filled with a dark blue sky glittering with gold stars (Photo 1–50). The only natural light inside was from small alabaster windows, which means the gold stars must have glittered beautifully in the light of candles or torches. The dark blue background is seen in many early Christian mosaics. The integration of the gold stars is a stepping-stone to the awe inspiring golden domes (Photo 1-49). St. Apollinare in Classe, just outside of Ravenna, features a lovely apse mosaic with religious imagery surrounded by lambs, stylized flow-

ers, and trees against a gold background (Photo 1–52). The Neonian and Arian Baptisteries (Photo 1–5) both feature wonderful treatments of water and transparency in the scenes of the baptism of Christ set against gold backgrounds.

The Byzantines had a standard set of images that included the lives of Christ and Mary as well as other stories from the Bible. While limiting the subject matter, this allowed mosaicists a surprising opportunity for individual expression of the different subjects. The late Byzantine period saw a more stylized approach and an elongation of the human form. The domes were filled with gold, and figures floated on them along with other symbolic imagery. The cathedral on the island of Torcello in Venice has several interesting mosaics that show this later period. The apostles in the apse, dated around 1100, are almost Cubist in their design. At the opposite end is a fascinating mosaic, primarily in red and black, of *The Last Judgment* (Photo 1–55). The damned are shown suffering among flames and snakes. This mosaic is believed to be a copy of the original. The floors, possibly dating from an earlier period, are a complex example of Cosmati work,

1–42 *Top Left:* **Turtle and Rooster (the struggle between darkness and light)**, fourth century c.e. Basilica, Aquileia, Italy. Photo by author.

1–43 *Top Center:* **Tomb of Crescenta**, fifth century c.e. Bardo Museum, Tunis, Tunisia. Photo by author.

1–44 *Top Right:* **Lapwing**, fourth century c.e. Basilica, Aquileia, Italy. Photo by author.

1–45 *Above Right:* **Floor**, fourth century c.e. Basilica, Aquileia, Italy. Photo by author.

1–46 *Top Left:* **The Saints** (detail), fifth century C.E. Archepiscopalian Chapel, Ravenna, Italy. Photo by author.

1–47 *Top Right:* **Monogram and Doves**, fifth century C.E. Archepiscopalian Chapel, Ravenna, Italy. Photo by George Fishman.

1–48 *Bottom Right:* **The Redeemer Treading on the Serpent** fifth century C.E. Archepiscopalian Chapel, Ravenna, Italy. Photo by author.

1–49 *Opposite Page, Top Left:* **Starry Ceiling**, fifth century C.E. Archepiscopalian Chapel, Ravenna, Italy. Photo by author.

1–50 *Opposite Page, Top Right:* **St. Laurence Approaching Martyrdom on the Flames**, fifth century C.E. Archepiscopalian Chapel, Ravenna, Italy. Photo by author.

1–51 *Opposite Page, Bottom:* **The Clipeus Supported by Four Angels**, fifth century C.E. Mausoleum Galla Placidia, Ravenna, Italy. Photo by author.

1–52 *Following Pages:* **Apse**, fifth century C.E. St. Apollinare in Classe, Italy. Photo by author.

which are mosaics worked in *opus sectile*, created from sections of marble (Photos 1–58 and 1–61).

Istanbul also has several examples of late Byzantine mosaics. Hagia Sophia was the largest church in the eastern world when it was built in the sixth century. After 1453, it became a mosque. Now a museum, the huge golden domes still contain many of the original mosaics from the ninth through the twelfth centuries (Photo 1–57). Other churches in Istanbul are also now museums. The Church of Christ in Chora (also known as the Kariye Camii) contains mosaic scenes from the

Bible created in a stylized fashion in the early fourteenth century. The image of the leper is especially engaging (Photo 1–60). Nearby, the Church of Theotokos Pammakaritos, or Fethiye Camii, is under restoration, and it contains mosaics that show wonderful artistry in depicting the human form (Photo 1–56).

While the creation of most mosaics was centered around the Mediterranean, pre-Columbian mosaics were being made in the areas encompassed by Peru and Mexico in the fifteenth century. Masks and jewelry were created using a thin cladding of tiny turquoise and coral tesserae. The British Museum has some wonderful examples. Interestingly, these early mosaics in the Western Hemisphere were used to decorate objects, as opposed to walls or floors.

In the meantime, the expansion of Islam spread intricately patterned tile mosaics to southern Spain and beyond (Photo 1–64). In China, pebble mosaic pavements were created along traditional subjects like flowers, vines, and other elements of nature. The dates for these mosaics are uncertain. In Thailand, large mosaic statues were made from small mirrors and tiles.

Mosaic art began to lose popularity with the arrival of the Renaissance. As painting styles became more naturalistic, mosaicists responded to the times and imitated that style. Historically, whenever mosaic art tried following a different medium—whether by copying paintings during Roman times or imitating

1–53 *Opposite Page: Empress Theodora*, fifth century C.E. San Vitale, Ravenna, Italy. Photo by author.

1–54 *Top:* **Facade of Porta Sant' Alipio**, thirteenth century C.E. San Marco, Venice. Photo by author.

1–55 *Center Right: The Last Judgment* (detail), twelfth century C.E. Basilica, Torcello, Italy. Photo by author.

1–56 *Left: Archangel Raphael*, twelfth century C.E. Fetihye, Istanbul, Turkey. Photo by author.

1–57 *Opposite Page:* **Emperor Constantine**, eleventh century C.E. Hagia Sophia, Istanbul, Turkey. Photo by author.

1–58 *Top:* **Cosmati Work Floor**, eleventh century C.E. Basilica, Torcello, Italy. Photo by author.

1–59 *Above Left:* **Ascension of Christ**, thirteenth century C.E. Church of St. Frediano, Lucca, Italy. Photo by author.

1–60 *Right:* **The Leper** (detail), 1320 C.E. Kariye Museum, Istanbul Turkey. Photo by author.

1-61 Top: Floor combining Cosmati work and tessellated mosaic, twelfth century C.E. Basilica dei Santi Maria e Donato, Murano, Italy. Photo by author.

1-62 Bottom: Elephant with Cloven Hooves, eleventh century C.E. Ganagobie, France. Photo by author.

1-63 Opposite Page: The Lamb on the Mount in the Chapel of St. Zeno, thirteenth century C.E. Basilica of St. Praxedes, Rome. Photo by author.

the Renaissance style—the outcome was unfavorable. While often these mosaics were examples of incredible technical expertise, the denial of the medium lost the essence of the mosaic because the material became subservient to the image. Creating a realistic painting in mosaic was extraordinarily difficult and expensive. During the Renaissance, it became evident that if a patron wanted a painting, he would probably commission a painting. It took many years before mosaics began to regain popularity.

During the sixteenth century, the Vatican Mosaic Workshop was established to create mosaic decorations. The workshop recreated many of the paintings in St. Peter's in a more durable medium. It eventually became one of the major centers for mosaic production. The workshop, which is the oldest continuously-running mosaic studio, produced over 25,000 colors of smalti to replace the painter's palette (Photo 1–70). Artisans still make the filati, or glass rods, that are used to create mosaics for papal gifts.

In the 1700s, micromosaics became popular as souvenirs for wealthy Europeans who took the grand tours of Europe. These small mosaics depicted postcard-like scenes of places such as Rome and Italy. The amount of minute detail in these small works is amazing. A micromosaic may contain several thousand tesserae in a square inch. You often need a magnifying glass to fully appreciate the workmanship of the artist. Sir Arthur Gilbert's collection of micromosaics, at Somerset House in London, contains many examples of this painstaking art. The pendant shown in Photo 1–67 is by Laura Hiserote, who restored many of the collection's micromosaics. This incredible piece is only 2.25 x 1.8 inches (57 x 46 mm) and contains almost 16,500 tesserae.

In the mid-1800s, a Venetian lawyer named Salviati is credited with introducing the indirect method of creating mosaic (Photo 1–68). This method involves creating the mosaic in reverse in the studio and then shipping the tessellated composi-

tions, which are glued to paper, for installation elsewhere. Though there has been much speculation about the Romans using the indirect method for creating emblemata (the central motifs inset into pavements), no clear evidence has yet confirmed the theory. Salviati's workshop became a commercial success by creating mosaics with this method (Photo 1–69). The method later allowed mosaic studios to recreate the designs of well-known artists, like Marc Chagall, for installation in architectural settings.

By the early nineteenth century, the folk art tradition of "memory vessels" began in the southern United States (Photo 1–72). These mosaics were primarily created by African-Americans who pressed broken china, coins, and other memorabilia onto a jar or vessel. The mosaics were placed on graves to ease the passing of a loved one. Various adaptations of memory ware created from found objects remain popular today.

The Art Nouveau movement originated in the late nineteenth century and brought a new fluidity to mosaic designs. Nature and natural forms were the basis for the style. Mosaics were used to make signs and decorate surfaces (Photo 1–71). Even Louis Tiffany created mosaics from stained glass. The Pasteur Institute in Paris houses the crypt of Louis Pasteur. It is clad in beautiful gold and glass mosaics. The twining of vines and flowers through the images are typical of the Art Nouveau style (Photo 1–73).

The modern development of mosaics as forms of individual expression began in the early 1900s in several locations. Barcelona saw imaginative and vibrant work from several sources. In 1909, the architect, Lluís Domènech i Montaner, completed the Palau de la Musica featuring a vibrant mosaic facade (Photo 1–74) as well as colorfully clad columns executed by Lluís Bru (Photo 1–75). The best-known mosaics in Barcelona, however, are those of architect Antoni Gaudí, who often worked with the assistance of Josep M. Jujol. His Casa Batlló, finished in 1906, features a mosaic facade

1–67 *Left:* **Laura Hiserote.** *Rite of Passage* (detail), 2000. 16,394 enamel glass threads mounted in 22k gold. Photo by Erica and Harold Van Pelt.

1–68 *Top Right:* Italian mosaicists working on sections of a cartoon using the indirect method. Pietrasanta, Italy. Photo by author.

1–69 *Bottom Center:* Partially completed cartoon of an indirect mosaic. Pietrasanta, Italy. Photo by author.

1–70 *Bottom Right:* Cases with selection of smalti colors. Vatican Mosaic Workshop, Rome. Photo by the author.

1–64 Top: **Islamic Tile Mosaic in the Harem**, sixteenth century C.E. Topkapi Palace, Istanbul, Turkey. Photo by author.

1–65 Above: **Vestibule of the Palantine Chapel**, eighteenth century C.E. Royal Palace, Palermo, Italy. Photo by author.

1–66 Right: **Facade Mosaic** (detail), seventeenth century C.E. San Marco, Venice. Photo by author.

1–76 Top: **Antoni Gaudí** (designer). Ceramic Facade and Roof, 1904–1906. Casa Battló, Barcelona, Spain. Photo by author.

1–77 Left: **Antoni Gaudí** and **Josep M. Jujol.** Undulating Benches, 1905–1914. Parc Güell, Barcelona, Spain. Photo by author.

1–78 Right: **Antoni Gaudí** and **Josep M. Jujol.** Lizard Fountain. Parc Güell, Barcelona, Spain. Photo by author.

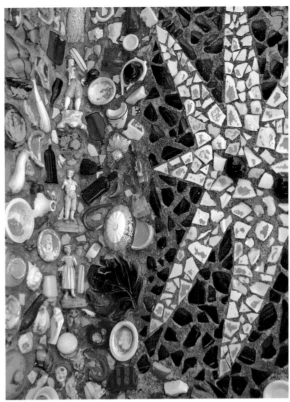

1–79 *Opposite Page:* **Raymond Isidore.** Wall of Chartres, 1938–1962. Maison Picassiette, Chartres, France. Photo by author.

1–80 *Top Left:* **Empress Teresa Cristina.** Seating Area, 1852. Princess Garden, Rio de Janeiro, Brazil. Photo by Henrique Gougon.

1–81 *Above:* **Antoni Gaudí** and **Josep M. Jujol.** Gate Building, 1905–1914. Parc Güell, Barcelona, Spain. Photo by author.

1–82 *Top Right:* **Raymond Isidore.** Detail of Wall at Maison Picassiette. Chartres, France. Photo by author.

1–83 *Center Right:* **Raymond Isidore.** In the Garden at Maison Picassiette. Chartres, France. Photo by author.

1–84 *Bottom Right:* **Antoni Gaudí** and **Josep M. Jujol.** Medallion from the Ceiling at Parc Güell. Barcelona, Spain. Photo by author.

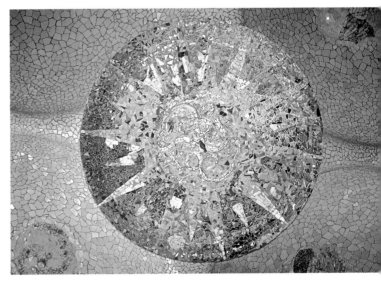

1–85 Top Left: **Raymond Isidore.** *Lady in the Garden*, 1938–1962. Maison Picassiette, Chartres, France. Photo by author.

1–86 Below Left: **Niki de Saint Phalle.** Interior of the Empress, 1978–1990. Il Gardena dei Tarocchi, Tuscany, Italy. Photo by author.

1–87 Below Right: **Niki de Saint Phalle.** *The Magician and the High Priestess*, 1978–1990. Il Gardena dei Tarocchi, Tuscany, Italy. Photo by author.

1–88 Bottom Right: **Niki de Saint Phalle.** *The Sun*, 1978–1990. Il Gardena dei Tarocchi, Tuscany, Italy. Photo by author.

1–89 Opposite Page: **Niki de Saint Phalle.** *The Emperor (The Castle)*, 1978–1990. Il Gardena dei Tarocchi, Tuscany, Italy. Photo by author.

1–90 Opposite Page, Top Left: **Nek Chand.** *The Rock Garden*, 1965–. Chandigarh, India. Photo by Carl Lindquist.

1–91 Opposite Page, Top Right: **Isaiah Zagar.** *The Painted Bride* (Front Entrance), 1991–1999. Philadelphia, PA. Photo by the artist.

1–92 Opposite Page, Bottom Left: **Isaiah Zagar.** *The Painted Bride* (Side Wall), 1991–1999. Philadelphia, PA. Photo by the artist.

1–93 Opposite Page, Bottom Right: **Simon Rodia.** *Watts Towers*, 1921–1954. Los Angeles, CA. Photo by author.

1–94 Top: *Barcelona Scene*, 1968. Liceu Metro Station, Barcelona, Spain. Photo by author.

1–95 Above: **Nek Chand.** *The Rock Garden*, 1965–. Chandigarh, India. Photo by Carl Lindquist.

1–96 Above: **Eduardo Paolozzi.** Tottenham Court Underground Station, 1984. Smalti and vitreous glass. London. Photo by author.

1–97 Right: **Melbourne Mural Studio.** *Skygarden* (in progress), 1989. Photo by David Jack.

1–98 Opposite Page: **Joan Miro.** *Dona i Ocell*, Barcelona, Spain. Photo by author.

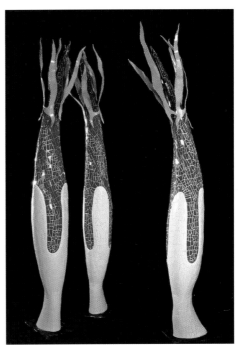

1–99 Opposite Page: **Ezio Frigerio** (designer) and **Akomena** (execution). Tomb of Rudolf Nureyev, 1996. Smalti and golds. Russian cemetery, St. Geneviève des Bois, France. Photo by author.

1–100 Left: **Marco Bravura.** *Ardea Purpurea Fountain*, 1999. Each monolith: 20 x 5 feet (6.2 x 1.5 m). Marble, smalti, golds, ceramic. Beirut, Lebanon. Photo by Maurizio Montanari.

1–101 Below Right: **Val Carroll.** *Unlikely Menage x 3*, 1993. 11 x 4 x 2.5 feet (3.4 x 1.2 x 0.8 m). Ceramic, steel, and concrete. Photo by the artist.

1–102 Bottom: **Haruya Kudo.** *The Fragrant Earth* (detail), 1992. Marble, smalti, golds. Photo by the artist.

Irina Charny. *Primavera,* 2002. 48 x 14 inches (122 x 36 cm). Glass, china, gold, millefiori, ceramic. Photo by Ben Charny.

MATERIALS AND TOOLS

MATERIALS

Amosaic is created from hundreds of tesserae, or individual pieces. The word originated with the Romans and initially meant "cube of marble or stone." Today, a tessera can be a piece of tile or smalti, marble or gold, a seashell or a bit of broken china. Contemporary mosaics are created from a huge variety of materials, which add excitement and texture. Your choices are limited only by the imagination.

Factors to consider when selecting materials include durability, thickness, color, light refraction, and ease of cutting. Check out local tile dealers, craft stores, and even thrift shops in your materials search. The Internet is now the best source for a wide selection. The amount of material that you need for each project in this book is not specified because requirements will vary depending on the size of the base and the materials chosen. Always buy 25% more than you think is needed. This allows for tiles that may not cut well and possible adjustments in color choices.

SMALTI

Smalti is the enameled glass used by the Byzantine to create fabulous wall and ceiling mosaics. It is considered the finest of mosaic materials and is prized for its purity of color, texture, and light-refractive

Above: A small selection of sample boards for mosaic materials. Photo by author.

2-1 The smalti storage room of Angelo Orsoni Srl in Venice. Notice the large oval "pizza" of smalti. Photo by author.

There are several aspects of smalti to consider if you decide to use it. Its purity of color and reflective quality make smalti an ideal choice for fine art and decorative mosaics. It is often left ungrouted for several reasons. Grouting smoothes out a surface, but smalti is prized for its uneven, hand-cut surface. In addition, the high-fire manufacturing process of smalti often leaves tiny air bubbles in the glass. This added uniqueness of the material will allow grout to get into its holes and make cleaning very difficult. Because smalti has sharp edges, it is a bad choice for floors, shower stalls, or anywhere that people might rub against. Its color intensity requires a careful eye to make sure the strong colors don't "take over" a mixed-material mosaic. A grainier version of smalti, called antico, is less light-refractive but its color palette is limited.

Smalti is most often shipped in bags of small, hand-cut brick-shaped tesserae. These can be cut smaller or left whole and fitted together. Larger pieces can also be special-ordered from Italy.

Filati, a subset of smalti, are used to create micromosaics. A filato is a long thin rod or cane of enameled glass. The rods are set vertically and cut to the desired depth. Working with filati is exacting work that can cause eyestrain. Using a magnifying glass and light combination is recommended.

qualities. Thousands of colors exist in smalti. The Vatican Mosaic Workshop has over 25,000. Current manufacturers in Italy and Mexico have palettes with hundreds of colors readily available. Smalti is manufactured in small color batches under exacting conditions by adding oxides to molten glass and then finishing it up as large flat "pizzas." The slabs are then cut into rods and nipped into small, irregular brick-shaped tesserae. Each piece of smalti has an individual, highly light-refractive surface. Like the Byzantine, contemporary mosaicists often press pieces of smalti into the adhesive at slightly different angles to emphasize the reflections. Controlling the depth of the cement allows for various effects, from "self-grouting" to deep grooves between the tesserae. Smalti may be set very tightly or further apart to allow the spaces to add a textural quality to the work.

VITREOUS GLASS

Vitreous glass (also know as Venetian glass) is a modern mosaic material that became popular in

2-2 Smalti.

the 1950s and 1960s. A wide color selection and consistent surface make this material especially useful for murals, signage, bathrooms, and tabletops. With the exception of reds and yellows, the colors are more subdued and less intense than smalti. Vitreous glass is suitable for outdoors and often used commercially for swimming pools and spas. This explains the extended range of blues, aquas, and greens. Beside the regular color spectrum, vitreous glass is also available with a blended, metallic effect running through the tiles or with a pearly, iridescent finish.

Mixing tiles from different manufacturers offers an expanded color selection while retaining a flat surface. The European-made vitreous glass has a less grainy appearance and is less brittle to cut. Consequently, it is more expensive. Color consistency can vary between manufacturers as well as between different production runs. Vitreous tiles are grooved on the back to enhance adhesion but they may also be used "bottom up." This gives an interesting texture but it is more difficult to grout. Edges are beveled on the back, which is helpful for going around corners or covering curved surfaces. The tiles are readily cut into small squares, triangles, or narrow strips.

Vitreous glass is manufactured all over the world, including Italy, Mexico, France, Venezuela, and China. It is pressed in molds, giving it a standard dimension of ¾-inch (20-mm) square and ⁵⁄₃₂-inch (4-mm) thickness. It is usually shipped in

sheets of 225 tiles (15 x 15), which is slightly more than a square foot (1.06 sq. ft/985 sq. cm). The tiles are glued facedown on brown paper. Before using, place the sheet facedown in a sink of hot water and the paper will float off in a few minutes.

Some manufacturers offer "tiny tiles" in a ⅜-inch (10-mm) square. This size can be very handy to use without cutting. But the regularity can also be a problem. A mosaic created from these small tiles can be somewhat sterile by resembling a grid or counted cross-stitch. Take care to keep the handmade, individual look that makes the art of mosaics so appealing.

CERAMIC TILE

Ceramic tile may be glazed or unglazed, frost-proof or susceptible to severe weather conditions. Unless you live in a balmy climate, be sure the ceramic tiles you use for exterior projects will hold up under extreme weather conditions. Unless a glazed tile is frost-proof, the backing can absorb moisture. In a hard freeze, that moisture expands and may pop the glaze off. Unglazed tile that isn't rated for outdoor use may crumble over time. When purchasing ceramic tiles for exterior projects, inquire whether the material is frost-proof. For example, most 4-inch (10-cm) square bathroom tiles are not weatherproof. They have a chalky back and should be limited to use on interior projects. An easy test to determine the durability of a tile is to place a drop of water on its back. The drop will stay on the sur-

2–3 Vitreous glass tiles.

2–4 Metallic blended and iridescent glass tiles.

2–5 Glazed and unglazed ceramic tiles.

face of a frost-proof tile but it will be absorbed on an interior-grade tile. Practice this test on known tiles and the difference will become apparent.

Glazed ceramic tile is available in a wide range of colors, adding variety to a mosaic. It also comes in a variety of surface decoration and may be light refractive. A glazed tile is composed of two materials: the surface glaze and the backing material. Glazed tile is trickier to cut as the two materials break at a different rate of tension. (See pages 87–88 for instruction on cutting glazed tiles.)

Unglazed ceramic tile is usually made of the same material throughout. It may be called a "solid body." This offers several advantages. Cuts to unglazed ceramic usually have cleaner edges and occasionally a tessera will be the perfect shape—if

2–6 Water test for frost-proof tile. The tile on the right is frost-proof.

only it were upside down. With a solid body tile, just flip it over. The tile is the same color throughout. The color range is expanded by mottled tones that resemble stone. Some solid body tiles are available with a clear glaze so that you can mix the shiny front surface and the matte backside for an interesting textural look.

Specialty ceramic tiles are also available. These include leaf shapes, hearts, tiny tiles, ovals, and other unusual designs. They can be purchased from craft shops or mosaic suppliers.

Some ceramic tiles are shipped in sheets that are formed by connecting the tiles with rubber dots on the back. When ordering ceramic tiles for mosaics, specify unmounted when possible.

2–7 Golds in various colors and textures created from 24k gold and sandwiched between two layers of glass.

Gold Smalti

Originally used prodigiously in Byzantine churches to awe the worshippers, gold smalti remain a beautiful, though extravagant, material for mosaics. They are made in small factories, primarily in Italy, from a 24k gold leaf sandwiched between a thin and thick piece of glass. Pavimento, the golds used for floors, have a thick, clear glass on top to prevent foot traffic from wearing through to the gold. Golds for artwork, walls, and ceilings (rivestimento) have thin glass on top to allow maximum reflection of the gold. Rivestimento smalti are usually backed by aqua or turquoise glass that makes the reverse very beautiful, too. The surface of gold smalti may be smooth or bumpy. Colors range from white gold to yellow gold to copper color or rose gold to more unusual colors.

STONE

Marble, slate, and other natural stones offer both permanence and texture. This can be seen in Roman floor mosaics. Primarily made of marble, they have lasted thousands of years.

Marble is very durable and comes in a wide range of natural colors. Tumbled or polished marble tesserae can be purchased by the square foot on mesh sheets that are ready for floor installation. Pull or soak the cubes off the mesh. You can use the cubes whole or cut them into smaller pieces. As an

2–8 Slate, marble tesserae, and rods.

alternative, use a wet saw to cut 12-inch (30-cm) square marble floor tiles into rods and then nip them to size. Note that some marble colors will be easier to cut after being soaked in water.

Slate will often have a variety of subtle color differences within a single piece. Cutting with a wet saw or breaking with a hammer and bolster can recycle old slate roofing tiles.

Many other stones and minerals work well in a mosaic, so experiment with several.

PEBBLES

Pebble mosaics have a long history beginning with black and white Greek mosaics. Today, a variety of colored pebbles are available. You can find them through landscape rock suppliers or even look for them in a parking lot. Pebbles and gravel add interesting textures to a mosaic.

2–9 Various shades of natural pebbles.

CHINA

Picassiette, or broken china mosaic, is extremely popular. The word *picassiette* is French for "stolen plate." You can gather the material for this kind of mosaic by recycling a broken heirloom or making use of garage sale and thrift store bargains. Break the china with a hammer or cut it with nippers.

Because plate centers and borders are customarily flat, they make great material for a mosaic. The footplate may be nipped or ground off. Broken china offers some unusual shapes. The cup handles can be a creative and fresh addition to a decorative mosaic.

Be aware that some china may not be frost-proof. Use the water drop test on an exposed edge to determine its durability for exterior use (see page 68).

2–10 Assorted china pieces.

2–11 Transparent, translucent, and opaque stained glass.

Gold accents on china, which are often applied after firing, may come off during grouting. Cover the gold areas with masking tape to protect them.

STAINED GLASS

Stained glass is becoming a more popular choice to use in mosaic. Like all materials, there are benefits and drawbacks. One of the benefits is that stained glass comes in a huge range of colors and, for the most part, it is very economical. (Though dichroic glass, a stunning metallic-looking stained glass, is somewhat expensive.) With the correct tools, stained glass is easy to cut into intricate shapes.

A drawback to stained glass is that it is a comparatively thin material that requires careful control of adhesive depth to ensure that enough space be left for grouting. There is also a tendency to use larger sections of glass that are cut to exact shapes, which loses some of the traditional feeling of a mosaic. Most stained glass is transparent or translucent, which is great for applying to a clear surface using a clear adhesive. However, when using over cement or wood, it means the adhesive and backing surface will show through. Do some experiments to understand the finished results. Brightness

may be dulled and color differences may become less apparent, depending on the surface under the glass. A white base enhances the colors and a black grout will give a stained-glass effect. Be sure the back of each piece is fully covered with adhesive. Otherwise, the grout can work under and look messy from the front. Also, be aware that clear materials will reveal any sketch or guidelines beneath.

Tumbling stained glass is a good safety precaution to follow before you begin working. This will remove most of the sharp edges. Use a small hobbyist's rock tumbler with a mixture of liquid soap and water, and tumble for a few hours. This smoothes the edges while keeping scratches to a minimum. Even after tumbling, be very careful when handling stained glass.

MIRROR

Mirror is a fun way to add a lot of interest and depth to a mosaic. You can get this material by using bits of a broken mirror or buying mirror tiles at a home-improvement store. These can be scored and cut just like stained glass but, again, be careful of the edges. Make sure the tiles are real mirror, not the plastic look-alike version. Some mirror tiles have a plastic backing that must be peeled off before cutting.

Mirror comes in a variety of thicknesses that can be matched to the surrounding material.

2–12 Plain, colored, and textured mirror.

Although it comes in a range of colors, like bronze- and gray-tinted mirror, these colors are more difficult to find. Mirror is subject to tarnishing, so use the correct adhesive and make sure the grout is sealed against moisture.

MARBLE GEMS

Flat-back marble "gems" have become very popular in the last few years. The color selection has expanded to over fifty choices. Different finishes include shiny, metallic, iridized, and frosted. The transparency varies among clear, translucent, and opaque. These gems can make the perfect eye for a fish or add a unique textural element. Be careful if you try to cut the gems, as they may shatter. Using wheeled cutters works best.

2–13 Marble gems.

ALTERNATIVE MATERIALS

The choice of alternative materials is extensive. Natural or man-made, these unusual elements can add excitement and personality to a mosaic. When deciding to use an unusual object, be sure to consider factors such as durability, permanence, and light refraction.

Looking for alternative materials is like hunting for a treasure. At anytime, anyplace, you may come across an object that inspires you. For example, a trip to the seashore offers a multitude of beach glass and seashells (but be sure that collecting the material will not be a detriment to the environment). Seashells can be fragile and may need to be protected by setting them deeply into cement.

2–14 Alternative materials including shells, beach glass, and abalone.

Mother-of-pearl and abalone shells add a beautiful, lustrous effect to a mosaic.

Think about recycling unusual materials for your mosaic. Watch faces, flattened cutlery, buttons, and other discarded objects are fun to integrate into a design. Be aware that some materials can add interest but may lack durability.

Easily accessible and low-cost materials, such as corks, beans, seeds, and pasta, are ideal tesserae for making a mosaic with children. Finishing these with a sealer or varnish will lengthen their life span.

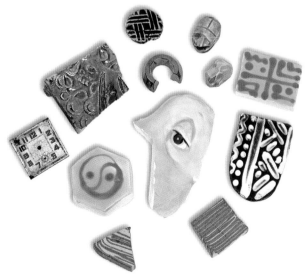

2–15 One-of-a-kind pieces, including handmade pottery, gems, scarab, and watch face.

ONE-OF-A-KIND

Unique ceramic tesserae and glass fusions can be created with minimal equipment. Take a class at a local arts center and learn to make custom tesserae.

It is a good idea to keep some plastic bags, a dustpan, a brush, and work gloves in the trunk of your car. You never know when the perfect new material may appear. A broken windshield in a parking lot can be an exciting find.

Keep in mind that although mixing different materials can make a fun and exciting mosaic, it can also make grouting harder. As the sponge cleans the grout off the high pieces, it pulls the grout onto the lower ones. This will make it take longer to clean up your mosaic. You may need to "excavate" the shallower tiles with a dental tool and then individually clean the low spots.

BASES

A finished mosaic represents hours of work. Using the wrong surface for your mosaic can shorten its life span. Many factors determine the choice of a base or substructure. One is the mosaic's intended use and location. For example, exterior projects need to be durable and weatherproof; large and heavy wall hangings shouldn't warp.

PLYWOOD

Plywood is great for indoor projects. It is not recommended for outdoor works since plywood will expand and contract under freezing conditions. Although marine grade plywood is treated to enhance durability under adverse conditions, it will not completely prevent it from rotting. Sealing helps (see pages 93–94) but the wood will still ultimately decay.

For indoor projects, choose plywood that is at least ⅝-inch (1.6-cm) thick in order to avoid warping. You should seal the wood with a PVA/water mix (see page 74).

MDF

Medium Density Fiberboard, commonly referred to as MDF, is an improved and concentrated particleboard. It is dense and heavy and will not warp. Despite its strength, don't ever use MDF for an outside project. It is made from compressed and glued pieces of sawdust and it will lose its integrity under damp conditions. MDF has a very smooth surface. Using a knife or nail to scratch the working side before sealing will add "tooth" to the surface, which will enhance adhesion.

CEMENT BACKER BOARD

Cement backer board is the ideal choice for flat, outdoor projects. It is manufactured from cement and fiberglass mesh. Many brands are waterproof, and it is most commonly used as a subsurface for shower walls. Backer board is available in large sheets of varying thickness. Another type of backer board is made by cladding cement over a meshcovered foam board. This type is much lighter in weight.

Scoring the surface and snapping along the scored line will give you straight cuts on a cement board. Curves can be cut using a jigsaw equipped with a masonry blade. As with all building materials, follow the manufacturer's instructions. Cutting cement board releases a lot of cement dust, so it is essential that you wear a dust mask or respirator.

If you are making a project, like a table, use a cement board that is a ½-in (1.3-cm) thick and make sure that the table bases have cross supports. This way, the surface will not flex and cause cracks in the grout.

POTTERY AND CEMENT

Terra-cotta pots and garden art make fun mosaic accents for the patio. But, like wood, terra-cotta can absorb moisture from the adhesive and weaken its bond with the tesserae. It may also cause grout to dry too quickly, which hampers the curing process. You can avoid this by sealing the terra-cotta with a PVA/water mix (see page 74) before applying the mosaic. When finished, apply a penetrating grout sealer to all the surfaces of the pot, inside and out. This prevents moisture from reaching the back of the mosaic and possibly causing mildew.

Cement birdbaths, stepping stones, and statuary come in a variety of shapes, styles, and sizes. When possible, avoid bases with intricate curves that may complicate the placement of tesserae as well as grouting.

FURNITURE

Applying mosaic to furniture transforms it into "fun-iture." Check the attic or make a trip to the thrift store for a creative and unusual base. Chairs, tables, and armoires are all popular choices, but the furniture must be solidly constructed to take the added weight of a mosaic surface. Otherwise, any flexing or warping can cause the pieces to pop out. Be sure to strip or scuff-sand any painted or varnished surface before you begin. Deep grooves and curliques can be filled with wood putty in order to make them easier to mosaic.

METAL

Metal objects can be covered using the appropriate adhesive. But if your mosaic is an outdoor project, the metal may contract and expand under temperature extremes. This causes the grout to crack and occasionally tiles may pop off. If possible, prepare the surface by fixing a wire mesh over the metal with screws and then apply a coat of cement. Apply the mosaic pieces and be sure to seal thoroughly after the grout cures. An easier alternative is to use epoxy adhesive.

MESH

Many tiles are shipped on mesh and are ready to press into the adhesive and then grout. The same principle works for creating mosaics on mesh. The tesserae can be glued directly to the mesh and installed later. Fiberglass mesh, commonly used when applying stucco, can be purchased from a building materials supplier.

PLEXIGLAS AND GLASS

Applying transparent or translucent materials to a Plexiglas or glass surface requires an adhesive that dries clearly. You can mix materials with different degrees of transparency to create interesting effects, but be sure any plastic used as a base is thick enough that it will not flex. If the surface flexes, all but the smallest tesserae may pop off.

READY-MADE FORMS

Craft and hobby stores are great sources of ready-made bases for mosaic projects. Birdhouses, trays, picture frames, and plaques are just some of the choices. It is better to select forms with flat surfaces rather than lots of routing and curves. This will make applying tile and grouting much easier.

ONE-OF-A-KIND

You can make custom three-dimensional mosaics by sculpting a Styrofoam block into the desired shape. It's best to do this outdoors and over a plastic tarp, since carving Styrofoam makes a huge mess that is difficult to clean. On large pieces, wrap the finished form with a soft, malleable wire mesh and secure it with wire pins and glue. (Don't use glue that contains solvents. It will dissolve the Styrofoam.) Then apply a layer of cement over the wire to serve as a base for applying the mosaic. Use cement-based adhesive to apply the tesserae and grout. The sculpture will be both stable and weatherproof. If the base is small, cement may be applied directly to the Styrofoam.

ADHESIVES

The choice of an adhesive will have a big impact on both the finished mosaic as well as your enjoyment in its creation. Exposure to the fumes and chemicals emitted by some adhesives as well as the possibility of skin irritation are things you need to be aware of. Always read the fine print and warning labels on the products used. There are several strong adhesives that clearly state they contain known carcinogens. The effects of extended and

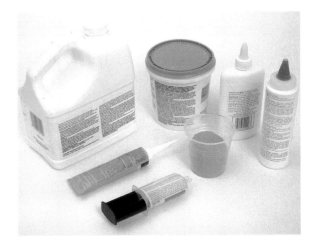

2–16 Adhesives. *Clockwise from top left:* admix, mastic, washable school glue, PVA glue, cement-based adhesive, epoxy, and silicone.

even brief exposure is not known, so caution is advised. Many good adhesives that don't have these problems are described here.

PVA

The best all-around glue is catalyzed PVA (polyvinyl acetates). PVA is a white, odorless, non-toxic glue that dries clearly. In Europe, PVA glues are easily found and may be labeled for exterior or interior use. In the United States and Canada, white glues aren't labeled as PVA and are not all the same quality. My favorite is WeldBond, a widely-available brand that is weather resistant and gets harder over time. Mix four- or five-to-one with water for sealing wood and terra-cotta projects. Used undiluted, it will stick tile and glass to wood, cement, pottery, metal, and more. It takes 24 hours to cure and become completely clear. Over time, the bond will continue to strengthen. The PVA may take longer to cure on large pieces of stained glass that are glued to flat glass. The lack of exposure to air lengthens the time required for the glue to turn clear.

CEMENT-BASED ADHESIVE

Cement-based adhesive, or thinset mortar, is a sticky, fine-grained cement sold in a gray or white color. Because it's waterproof, thinset is a perfect choice for a mosaic that may be exposed to moisture. It's ideal for fountains, showers, and outdoor statuary. Many mosaicists work exclusively with thinset. You can create a feeling of freedom and interesting textures by allowing the mortar to squish up between the tiles. For added flexibility and durability, mix the mortar with admix (liquid latex admixture) instead of water. Note that some thinsets already have an additive in the dry mix and should be mixed with water. Some of these remain slightly flexible after curing, which makes them an ideal choice for outdoor use.

TILE MASTIC

Mastic is a very sticky, paste-like tile adhesive. It comes premixed in a container and can be applied with a craft stick or palette knife. Mastic provides maximum slip resistance on vertical surfaces and,

thereby, holds the tesserae immediately in place. It can be a little messy and difficult to control its thickness when you're trying to maintain good grout lines. Use mastic for indoor applications only where it will not be exposed to moisture. It is not recommended for use on floors, as it may become brittle and break down under pressure.

EPOXY

Epoxy is a very strong, waterproof, and permanent adhesive that comes in two parts: hardener and resin. Mixing equal parts of the two produces a chemical reaction that bonds surfaces together. Other than the odor (read the label), the biggest problem is mixing it thoroughly. The hardener must be blended throughout or the epoxy may not harden. So, even when it seems thoroughly blended, stir the mixture some more. Also, be sure to use fresh epoxy. If opened tubes have been in the drawer for a while, toss them out, and buy some new ones. New versions of epoxy advertise a quick-setting time, which is handy for working on vertical surfaces.

SILICONE

Silicone adhesive is a chemical polymer that is waterproof, flexible, and clear. It is ideal for attaching glass to glass. Be sure any Plexiglas surface is thick enough to avoid flexing. Silicone is so flexible it will move with the base and allow the tesserae to pop off.

WASHABLE SCHOOL GLUE

Washable school glue is used to create a mosaic using the indirect method (see page 116). The fact that it is completely water-soluble makes it a good choice for working in reverse.

GROUT

Grout is a cement-based mixture used to fill the interstices (or joints) between tiles and prevent moisture from reaching the adhesive and base support. It has no strength or adhesive qualities of its own. It acts only as a space filler. Grout is available in several forms, including dry and premixed. Always wear gloves when grouting and cleaning up.

Grout is also available in many colors, including some intense shades. There are several distinct advantages to using a manufacturer's color whenever possible. Grout dries considerably lighter than its wet appearance, so it would be very difficult to match a custom grout color. It is also better to use a manufacturer's color grout when working on a large mosaic in stages. You will not have to worry about having mixed too little grout in your first batch and possible repairs will be easier later on.

Sanded grout is the correct choice for most projects. The sand adds integrity to the grout, making it stronger and preventing shrinkage. Use sanded grouts for joints up to ½ inch (1.3 cm) wide. Although it is coarser than unsanded grout, you can avoid scratching any delicate mosaic surfaces by cleaning carefully.

Sanded grout is usually sold dry in a box or bag. Store any unused grout in an airtight container to preserve its quality. Most brands contain a polymer additive that improves the grout's flexibility, color retention, and water resistance. Mix the polymer-enhanced grouts with water. If a grout lacks the polymer additive, then use a liquid latex admixture instead of water.

Unsanded grout should only be used for joints of ⅛ inch (3 mm) or less. (Some brands suggest ¹⁄₁₆ inch (1.2 mm) or less). Because it lacks internal integrity, unsanded grout will often shrink below the tile surface if it is used in joints wider than the recommended spacing. Even worse, this shrinkage may cause the grout to crack and pull towards the sides of the joint. Premixed grout is usually unsanded and subject to these same problems.

Epoxy grouts can be used on mosaics that are subject to moisture or extreme conditions. Most epoxy grouts are waterproof and will withstand industrial temperatures. They are usually packaged in three parts: a resin, a hardener, and an aggregate. They are rather difficult to work with and to clean off the tiles. Before deciding to use epoxy grout, do a grout test on a small sample mosaic.

TOOLS
NIPPERS AND CUTTERS

The most commonly used tile nippers are called side biters, because the nippers only clip the edge of the tile. (More on cutting in the Techniques chapter, see page 83.) Side biters are inexpensive and invaluable. Some models are made from a

2–17 Tools. *Clockwise from top:* pro scorer/breaker, hammer, running pliers, glass scorer, handheld scorer/breaker, side biters, wheeled cutters, double-geared nippers (small and large).

2–18 Hammer and hardie.

You may want to remove the set pin to allow the cutters to open wider for different materials. With wheeled cutters, two perfect triangles can be cut from a single vitreous glass tile almost every time, and four thin strips can be cut rather than only three if you are using side biters. Keep the side biters handy, however, for curved cuts and trimming beveled edges.

Double-geared precision nippers provide extra leverage when cutting extremely hard material. They come in two sizes but both are limited by the jaw's top hinge. While they have extensive adjustments for tile widths, these nippers can only fit a tile at a maximum depth of ⅜ inch (nearly 1 cm). This works well on certain ceramic tiles but not as well on glass. The double-geared nippers are also great to work with if you have weak hand strength. These precision cut nippers manufactured by the L.S. Starrett Company are comparatively expensive and must be special ordered. A nice feature is that replacement blades are available.

A professional tile scorer/breaker can cut ceramic tiles down to a manageable size. This device scores a line across the surface of the tile. Pushing down on the handle presses the tile between the breaking bar and a hard metal ridge. The tile then snaps along the scored line.

To cut stained glass or mirror, use a glass scorer and running pliers. The smoothest cuts are made

2–19 Wet saw and bricklayer's bolster.

higher-quality metal and will hold a sharp edge longer. While it may not be the perfect tool for all jobs, side biters are the one nipper that is a must have. They come with a spring that spreads apart the handles after each squeeze. Some mosaic artists remove this spring in order to have more control, but it's really a matter of personal preference.

Wheeled mosaic cutters are great for vitreous glass tiles and they may also be used on stained glass, smalti, and some ceramic or china. These really are cutters, not nippers. Two versions are on the market: one with stationary wheels and the other with wheels that turn and wobble slightly. It is better to purchase the cutters with stationary wheels, as the cuts are straighter and more consistent. My favorite brand is Leponitt. When the wheels get dull, just use an Allen wrench to loosen them, turn the wheels slightly, and then retighten.

2–20 Small tools. *Clockwise from top left:* sculpting spatulas, dental picks, pottery needles, tweezers, craft sticks, utility knife, palette knives.

when the scorer is used with a little oil. Some scorers have a reservoir that holds the oil. After scoring, the running pliers will safely break the glass along the scored line.

A hammer and hardie have been traditionally used by the Italians to cut tesserae. A hardie is a very sharp chisel point usually set into the top of a log at about knee height. A piece of marble or smalti is held against the edge of the hardie. A sharp tap of the hammer opposite the hardie edge sends a fracture through the marble to create a tessera. A hammer and hardie may be purchased in Italy or on the Internet. Their use is somewhat uncommon in the United States since most jobs can be accomplished with nippers. But if you're working with very hard marble, then a hammer and hardie becomes a valuable addition to your studio.

A wet saw cuts both marble and ceramic tiles with a minimum of effort, though it makes a big mess. Water sprays over the spinning diamond blade (and elsewhere) to keep the blade from overheating while it is cutting tough materials. A wet saw is especially useful for cutting marble floor tiles into rods that can then be nipped. Be sure that the electrical outlet used for the wet saw has a ground fault circuit breaker. Also, wear safety glasses when you're working with a wet saw. Be extremely careful when you are pushing the tile against the blade. Using a push stick is a good safety habit. Also, wearing an apron (or a big plastic trash bag) will help

keep you dry. A diamond band saw can be used to cut intricate shapes.

A bricklayer's bolster is a very wide chisel used with a mallet or regular hammer. This is useful for reducing large pieces of stone down to a size that can be nipped. Be sure to purchase one with a hand guard to avoid injury.

SMALL TOOLS

Dental picks are useful for moving tiles around and adjusting a tessera's position. Tweezers allow the removal of a single piece without disturbing the others around it. A potter's needle is great for cleaning excessive adhesive from grout lines and unplugging glue bottles. Other types of dental tools and

2–21 Garden sieve for washing tiles.

sculptor's spatulas are good and handy additions to a toolbox. A utility knife is ideal for cutting sections when creating a mosaic on mesh (see pages 122-123) or in the indirect method (see page 116). Use one with a retractable blade for safety.

2–22 Top: Design tools. *Clockwise from top left:* large compass, colored pencils, small compass, rulers, right angle, triangles, china marker, pencil, permanent marker, eraser.

2–23 Above: Grouting and mounting tools. *Clockwise from top:* bucket, sponge, bowl, trowel, spreader, spatulas, rubber floats, notched spreader.

An artist's palette knife that is shaped like a small trowel is ideal for mixing and applying thinset. The angle of the handle allows you to work over existing tiles. The trowel shape offers a pointy end for applying adhesive into small spaces. A wooden craft stick is a disposable alternative for spreading mastic or thinset.

Another useful accessory is a turntable or Lazy Susan. When working on a three-dimensional piece, it's handy to be able to swing it around easily. Get one that will support heavy objects.

A flat garden sieve is very handy for soaking vitreous glass tiles off their paper backing. Place the sieve in a sink with a few inches of hot water. Place a sheet of tiles facedown in the sieve. Wait for the paper to float to the top, then simply pick the sieve up. The water drains away and the tiles can be spread over some newspaper to dry.

DESIGN TOOLS

You may need a variety of drawing tools when creating your design. Regular and colored pencils, permanent marker, china marker, and an eraser

2–24 An organized studio with good lighting, ample working surface, and easy access to tools and materials.

help get the drawing right. Rulers, compasses, right angles, and triangles are great when you're in doubt about your drawing ability.

GROUTING AND MOUNTING TOOLS

Grouting tools include a rubber float, spatulas, sponges, grooved spreader, and trowel. Use the rubber float to lightly smack an indirect mosaic (see page 120) into the adhesive or to spread grout into the joints. Spreaders and rubber gloves also work well for spreading grout. A spatula is good for mixing and distributing grout. Be sure any grout bowls or buckets are a flexible plastic. Sponges specifically made for removing grout may be purchased from the hardware store. These can be cut down for use on very small mosaics. It will make cleanup a lot easier. A grooved spreader or trowel is used when applying adhesive to floors, walls, and other large installations.

STUDIO SETUP OR WORKSPACE

A well-designed workspace makes creating mosaics a safe and enjoyable experience. Studios range in size from a card table in the den to a dedicated room. Though the needs are met in different ways, the fundamentals remain the same. Basic physical requirements include hard floors, lighting, ventilation, access to water, and lots of storage space. While the basics are essential, don't forget art will be created here. Use colors and images on the walls that inspire you. I like being surrounded by the colors of mosaic materials in clear containers. Background music is nice and a shelf with art books and technical references can turn break time into productive time.

Ideally, your setup should be in an area used solely for making mosaics. Nipping tile is messy and projects may take some time to complete. To be able to stop working for a while without putting

everything away is a welcomed option. While a spare bedroom may be tempting, avoid working over carpeting at all costs. Drop cloths and plastic sheeting help but small shards invariably find their way underfoot. Kitchen areas should also be avoided for the same reason. It is not safe to prepare food in an area where glass and tiles have been cut.

Natural light is important for working with colors and judging tonal changes. Setting up near a window or under skylights is ideal. Indirect light is best, as many mosaic materials are very shiny. A drawing-table lamp on an extendable arm lengthens working hours into the evening. Choose one with a two-bulb system. These have a circular fluorescent bulb around an incandescent daylight-adjusted bulb.

> **Tip:** *Resealable plastic food bags come in various sizes and are great for storage. The small bags can keep pieces of cut tile that are leftover from your projects. Keep the bag on top of the tile's color canister so that you can easily find the little tile pieces without having to fish for them. Larger bags are good for keeping custom-mixed grout powder, but be sure to label each bag with the project's name.*

Good ventilation is also essential. Cements and grouts are dusty, some adhesives are malodorous, and cutting tile disperses shards and dust. A ceiling fan and access to fresh air help alleviate these problems.

Easy access to water makes grouting and cleaning much easier. A laundry-size utility sink is great for soaking tiles off paper backing. However, never allow grout or cement residue to go down the drain. It will ultimately clog up and require a visit from the plumber. Cleanup should be done outside with a hose.

Storage often becomes the biggest issue when creating mosaics. As new materials are acquired, space becomes more precious. Lots of strong shelving and see-through containers not only make materials accessible but the colors and textures

serve as a source of inspiration. Clear plastic canisters with snap-on lids are ideal and available in a variety of sizes. Labeling these makes ordering and restocking materials easier. Grouts and cements are easily stored in plastic bulk-food storage containers. A restaurant supply store is a good source for a variety of sizes. Labeling grout containers is especially important, as grout colors look very different when dry.

A large worktable is needed for actually working on a mosaic. This can be the standard table height or taller. (A taller worktable will allow you to work standing or sitting.) My primary workspace is two tall tables set at right angles. The larger table is ideal for actually creating the mosaic as well as any materials currently being used. The side table provides an area for cutting tiles, tools, and more materials. This also helps keep shards and dust away from the mosaic in progress. Working with materials and tools in easy reach eliminates unnecessary motions. The side table can also be used for planning and drawing mosaic designs.

For sitting, I prefer a stool rather than a chair. Whichever you choose, be sure that it is comfortable, the right height, and ergonomically sound. Adjustable back support and swiveling are important features. Don't use a chair with arms, because it will interfere with nipping tile.

SAFETY

Safety should always be a consideration when working with mosaics. A little caution and thought can prevent accidents as well as make the creative experience more comfortable and enjoyable.

Safety glasses come in many styles and sizes. You should wear them whenever you are working with nippers, wet saws, or other cutting equipment. Cutting tesserae sends lots of little shards and splinters flying around. Although working from a proper cutting position (see page 85) can reduce the number of pieces hitting your face, it will not keep all of them away. To avoid injury, find a pair of safety glasses that are comfortable.

A mask can alleviate a lot of the dust and fumes you may inhale when cutting glass or working with

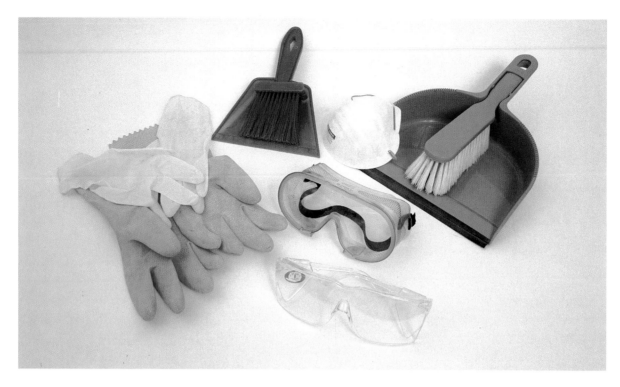

2–26 Safety equipment. *Clockwise from top left:* small brush and pan, dust mask, large brush and pan, safety glasses, latex and rubber gloves.

Tip: *It's important to keep the surface of the mosaic base clean so that maximum adhesion is possible. A 2-inch (5-cm) wide, soft paintbrush is ideal for cleaning around the tesserae of a work in progress. Just brush any splinters or shards into a dustpan.*

adhesives. You should always wear a mask when you are handling dry adhesive materials, such as grout and thinset. Since the adhesive hardens when moist, it can damage your lungs if you inhale it. If you are using glue with strong fumes, you may even consider wearing a respirator mask. It is not very expensive, but it should be fitted by a professional.

Wearing gloves will protect your skin from the alkali in the grout and mortar. If exposed, wash the area thoroughly and rub with vinegar. The acidity in the vinegar will restore the pH balance. Gloves will also make cleanup easier.

Always be careful when handling mosaic mate-

rials, since edges can be very sharp. Keep a dustpan and small brush for cleaning up the shards and splinters from your work area. Although it is the natural inclination to brush them off the work surface with your hand, little splinters are actually very hard to remove once they're in you. In addition to a dustpan and brush, an industrial grade handheld vacuum is great for cleanups. I also always keep a broom by my worktable for the crunchy bits that are under my feet. And always brush out your chair before returning to work. It can be very embarrassing to get out splinters that you have sat on.

Finally, get up often and move around. This is important for several reasons. Mosaic is fascinating and absorbing work. It's very easy to sit for hours without realizing it and then become stiff and achy afterwards. Cutting tiles is a repetitive motion and should be done in short stretches. Moving around also helps you look at the mosaic from different angles and distances. Mosaic is all about the sense one's eye makes out of all the bits and pieces. A different perspective can point out design flaws or happy accidents with light and texture.

TECHNIQUES

CHAPTER

Envisioning a mosaic design and bringing it to life becomes easier when the basic skills of shaping and assembling the tesserae are understood. Many of the techniques covered here are essential for beginning mosaicists while others may help experienced mosaicists reach a more advanced level.

Creating a mosaic is like solving a puzzle. Mastering various techniques allows the mosaic artist to not only "solve" the puzzle but to control the shape of the pieces. This chapter offers instructions in cutting and shaping the tesserae, how to place them, working with grouts and adhesives, and finishing the mosaic. But it is important to understand that there is usually more than one way to do something. If you've found a good method that works, then use it.

SHAPING THE TESSERAE

One of the first questions beginners always ask is "How do I cut tiles?" While the process is commonly referred to as "tile cutting," it is really "tile nipping." A mosaicist doesn't actually cut tiles but rather controls a fracture. A tile wants to break in the easiest way possible, but the easiest way usually doesn't result in the desired shape. The more cutting techniques you master, the greater "vocabulary" you have to work with. This will make things both easier and harder, because the bigger your vocabulary, the more complex your thoughts.

Understanding how the tools work and how the various sorts of

Above: Mosaic illustrating the use of the hammer and hardie at Scuola Mosaicisti del Friuli in Spilimbergo, Italy. Photo by author.

materials break make it possible to shape the tesserae with minimum effort. For instructional purposes, unglazed ceramic tiles are covered first, then other materials and variations.

First, look at the jaws of a basic tile nipper (or side biter) when it is closed (Photo 3–1). Note that they don't meet fully but rather leave a gap. If the jaws closed completely, you would be crushing the tile rather than nipping it. For the same reason, only a small part of the tile is covered by the side biter when nipping. If the jaws cover too much of the tile surface, nipping would become crushing and it would require a great deal of brute strength. By applying pressure on a small amount of the tile at

3–2 One side of the side biters has an overhang.

should use this technique.

Hold the nippers at a side view and look at the flat profile of the top of the jaws. How the top edge lines up with the tile determines the angle of the cut. If the top edge is parallel with the tile edge, the cut should be straight across (Photo 3–3). If angled, the cut should follow that angle (Photo 3–4).

BASIC STEPS

Sitting in a proper position and knowing how to apply pressure for nipping will make the process both safer and less tiring.

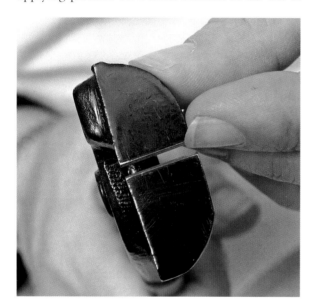

3–1 The jaws of the nippers don't meet.

its edge, you create a fracture across the surface. This technique allows you to cut a lot of tesserae without tiring. The trick is to learn to direct the fracture in order to control the resulting shape.

Now look at the nippers from a side view (Photo 3–2). Note that the jaws stick out on one side while the other is flat. The side with the overhang is the primary cutting surface. Cutting with this side is called "nipping." Certain cuts require using the center part of the jaws. This is called "nibbling." Occasionally, the flat or backside is used. The term for this is "backbiting." A small percentage of mosaicists cut primarily with the backside. If this works best for you then, by all means, you

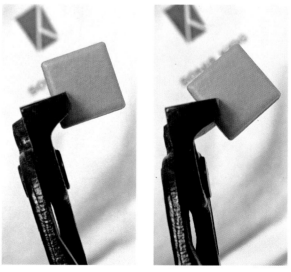

3–3 *Above Left:* Align the top of the nippers parallel with the top of the tile for a straight cut.

3–4 *Above Right:* Position the nippers at an angle on the tile.

1. Put on safety glasses.

2. Sit with your forearm relaxed on your thigh and lean slightly forward (Photo 3–5). Keep your arm relaxed and fairly straight so that your full strength can go into the cut. (A bent elbow binds up some of your strength and will require more hand pressure.)

3. Hold the nippers at the end of the handles to allow for maximum leverage and easier cutting. Position them so that the pressure is exerted from the meaty base of the thumb rather than the soft "vee" between the thumb and forefinger (Photo 3–6). Whether you are left- or right-handed, the overhang side of the nippers should point to the center.

4. Hold the tile in the opposite hand. Position about ⅛ inch (3 mm) of the jaws on the edge of the tile.

5. For a cut straight across the tile, align the top edge of the nippers parallel with the top edge of the tile.

6. Position your thumb and forefinger of the opposite hand across from the nippers (Photo 3–7).

7. At the same time that you firmly squeeze the handles of the nippers, squeeze the opposing thumb and forefinger at the point where the fracture should go. Pinching the edge of the tile as the nippers pinch the other edge will direct the fracture straight across the tile from tension point to tension point (Photo 3–8).

CONVEX AND CONCAVE SHAPES

Cutting convex and concave shapes are easy once the process is understood. To cut a circle, first "nibble" off the four corners using the center of the jaws (Photo 3–9). The result is an octagon. Continue nibbling off the sharp corners until you create a circle or oval (Photos 3–10 and 3–11).

Creating a tessera with a concave edge is a little trickier. Because a tile will always fracture along

3–5 Proper cutting position with arms down and wrist straight.

3–6 Hold the nippers by the ends of the handles for maximum leverage. Squeeze with the base of your thumb.

3–7 Position the nippers on the edge of the tile with your finger and thumb opposite.

3–8 Squeeze the nippers with one hand and pinch the opposite edge of the tile.

Tips:

1. Always keep the nippers down by your knees when you cut. This will keep the little shards and bits of fractured tile away from your face.

2. If nipping becomes difficult, you may be holding the nippers up too high and with a bent elbow, which requires too much hand strength. Or your hand may not be positioned at the end of the handles, which gives up the advantage of leverage. Return your forearms to your thighs and move your grip back down to the end of the handles. If the shape of the tesserae becomes a little off, double-check the angle of the nippers on the tiles. If you are cutting a tough exterior tile, then use double-geared nippers. It will be less tiring.

3. Cut the tiles over a shallow cardboard box to catch the shards and dust. Use a wide plastic tape to seal the corners and reinforce the top edges of the box. This won't entirely eliminate the cleanup afterwards, but it certainly helps. Also, wearing an apron will make cleaning up easier.

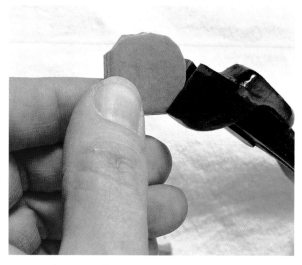

3–10 Cut the corners off the corners.

3–11 Smooth the circle edges.

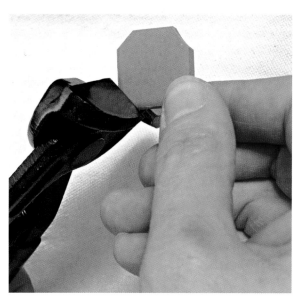

3–9 Start cutting a circle by nipping the four corners off a square.

3–12 To create an inset cut, begin by backbiting a small sliver.

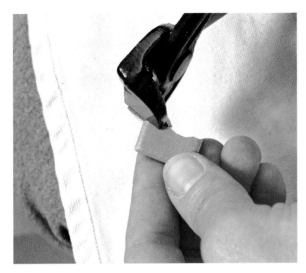
3–13 Nip a small sliver from the other side.

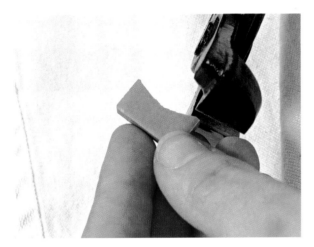
3–14 Work back and forth, creating a concave surface.

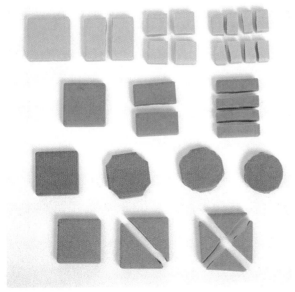
3–15 Sample cuts.

Tip: *When cutting a difficult piece, hold the tile over the empty space where it needs to go, check the needed angle, and make that cut. Hold it over the space again and cut the next angle. Continue in this manner of breaking it down to a manageable task. The same concept works for creating difficult sections of a mosaic. Just break them down to smaller tasks.*

the easiest line, begin the cut by "backbiting" the smallest bit from the tile's edge (Photo 3–12). If you try to take off too much, it's easier for the tile to break all the way across. After the first sliver is off, use the front of the nippers to take off a sliver from the other side (Photo 3–13). Continue working back and forth, backbiting and nipping a little bit at a time until the desired inset is made (Photo 3–14).

All this requires practice, but it will soon become second nature. Nipping, nibbling, and backbiting allow you to cut any needed shape. Different kinds of tile, different colors of the same tile, and even different color batches may cut differently. With experience, the necessary adjustments in pressure and position become automatic.

GLAZED TILES

Glazed tiles are trickier to cut because they consist of two materials: the body of the tile and the glazed surface. This requires directing the tension through materials of different strength and composition. Before I try to nip a large glazed tile into small tesserae, I first cut it down to a manageable size. Otherwise, the tile will probably break off in a curve towards the edge—the easiest way for it to go. Always work down by halves. This keeps an equal amount of tension on either side of the break.

The fastest way to cut large tiles down to a size appropriate for hand nipping is to use a pro scorer/breaker. There are various sizes and models, but they all work on the same principle. There is a sharp wheel for scoring, a curved breaking bar for applying pressure to either side of the scored line over the metal ridge, and a handle for directing it all. The scorer/breaker works best on glazed ceramic wall tiles and thin exterior tiles. Thick ones, like floor tiles, require a wet saw.

Using a scorer/breaker:
1. Position the tile against the back of the scoring area. Rest the wheel against the top of the tile's front edge (Photo 3–16).

2. Apply a slight downward pressure while sliding the handle forward, in effect scratching across the top of the tile (Photo 3–17). Only a slight score line is necessary (Photo 3–18). Applying too much downward pressure will cause the cut to craze and break with an uneven edge.

3. After scoring, make sure the handle is all the way forward and the wheel is in the well, not over the tile. Only score a tile once. Multiple score lines will cause bad breaks as the tile doesn't know which line to break along. Also any score lines or chips in the surface of a glazed tile will collect grout and adversely affect the finished look of a mosaic.

4. Position the breaking bar flat against the tile's surface and press down sharply. The tile will snap cleanly along the score line (Photo 3–19).

5. After the tiles are cut down, nip the tessera using the technique described on pages 84–85 (Photos 3–20 and 3–21). Pinching with the opposing thumb and forefinger is especially helpful with glazed tile.

NOTE: *While the scorer/breaker is great for scaling down large tiles, it will not work for cutting small tesserae. There must be enough room on either side of the score line for the bar to apply pressure and snap the tile. If scored too narrowly, the tile will break off in a curve.*

VITREOUS GLASS TILE AND OTHER MATERIALS
Vitreous glass tile can be cut using the basic shaping techniques but with a few additional instructions. The back of the tile has a ridged surface and a beveled edge. Making the first cut perpendicular

3–16 Position tile under wheel of pro scorer/breaker.

3–17 Hold tile while scoring lightly across the surface.

3–18 Tile with score line.

3–19 Snap the tile by pressing sharply on the breaker bar.

3–20 After scoring and snapping, the ceramic tile is a manageable size for nipping.

3–21 Position the nippers on the edge of the tile a and cut it in half.

to the ridges usually results in a better edge. Cutting parallel to the ridges often causes the tile to break unevenly. Sidebiters are essential for trimming edges or working on the beveled edge. If you are cutting a lot of vitreous glass, the wheeled mosaic cutters are a valuable tool. Note that these are cutters, not nippers, so the wheels are positioned over the center of the tile rather than on the edge (Photos 3–22 and 3–23). Hold the tile by the edges with your opposite hand so that it doesn't turn under the wheels. Then squeeze the cutters. The tile cuts easily. The wheeled cutters are better than side biters for cutting out triangles and long slender shapes (Photo 3–24).

Stained glass and mirror are most often cut using stained glass cutting tools. The principle is the same as the scorer/breaker. Use a glass cutter to score the surface and running pliers to snap it (Photos 3–25, 3–26, and 3–27). You can cut straight lines and curves with these tools. Then use the wheeled cutters to nip smaller tesserae from the

3–23 Then cut into quarters.

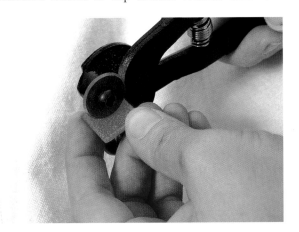

3–22 Use wheeled cutters to cut vitreous glass tile in half by positioning the wheels in the center.

3–24 Cut vitreous glass tile into triangles by positioning the wheeled cutters on the diagonal and holding the tile by the edges so it doesn't turn under the wheels.

3–25 Use the glass scorer and metal rule to score mirror or stained glass. Hold the scoring head perpendicular to the surface.

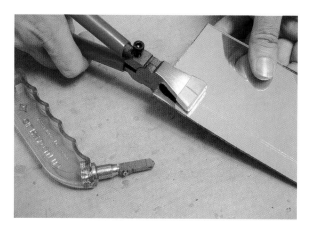

3–26 Position the running pliers by aligning the center mark with the scored line running pliers.

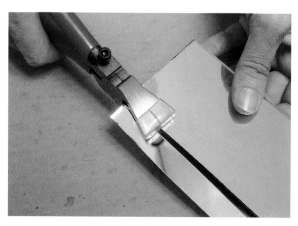

3–27 Snap with running pliers.

strips. Just be very careful about glass slivers.

Smalti and marble are often nipped with side biters though a hammer and hardie can also be used. The hardie used for smalti has a narrower edge than the one used for marble, though both work the same way. The hardie is usually embed-

ded in the top of a large log or wooden stand. With your thumb and forefinger, hold the material to be cut across the edge of the hardie. Position the hammer edge above the material, opposite the hardie (Photo 3–28). A small swing of the hammer delivers a sharp strike on the top edge, sending a fracture through the material against the opposing edge. Ideally, the hammer and hardie don't actually meet, so their edges stay sharp. This takes lots of careful practice as the edges are sharp, the hammer is heavy, and your fingers are soft. Wear safety glasses when you are working with a hammer and hardie. It is messy, so be sure to sweep up often.

An economical alternative to precut marble tesserae is square marble floor tiles. Using a tile wet saw, cut the floor tile into $1/2$ inch (1.3 cm) to $3/4$ inch (1.9 cm) wide strips. These will have a highly polished surface on top and a smooth, honed surface underneath. Use nippers or hammer and hardie to cut the tesserae to the size needed. This exposes the "riven" edge that is rough and textured, which is the natural beauty of the marble. (Note that the riven edge is difficult to clean if grouted.) Mixing the three surfaces can add interest and extend the color variations.

Creating china tesserae can be done several ways with varying levels of control. The easiest is to put the plate in the fold of a newspaper with the curved-side down. Cover it with the newspaper and place it on a concrete floor or other solid surface. (A table has too much give, so the breaks won't be sharp.) Give the newspaper a sharp whack with a hammer over the raised rim of the plate (see Photo 6–1 on page 128). Lift a corner of the paper and check your progress until the pieces are the size you want. Pick up the newspaper by the corners and shake. All the little shards will go to the bottom and you can carefully pick out the larger pieces. Throw the paper away with the small shards wrapped inside.

Using nippers or wheeled cutters will give you more control over the shape and size of the china pieces. Still, it's difficult to get exact shapes. The curves in the china make it unpredictable. It's best to treat it the same as glazed tile: work your way down to a manageable size by halves.

THE PHILOSOPHY OF TILE NIPPING

There are many ways to approach tile nipping. Some mosaicists will nip each tessera as it is needed while others will cut up all the pieces before starting work. I like to create an "inventory" of tesserae to choose from and then I cut any special shapes as needed. Having a lot of tesserae on hand helps me develop a rhythm while I lay them down. Be sure and replenish the stock as you go along. It's not uncommon to start using some of the slightly odd pieces that are left as inventory gets low. A mosaic with a wonderful rhythm will

3–28 The proper position for using a hammer and hardie.

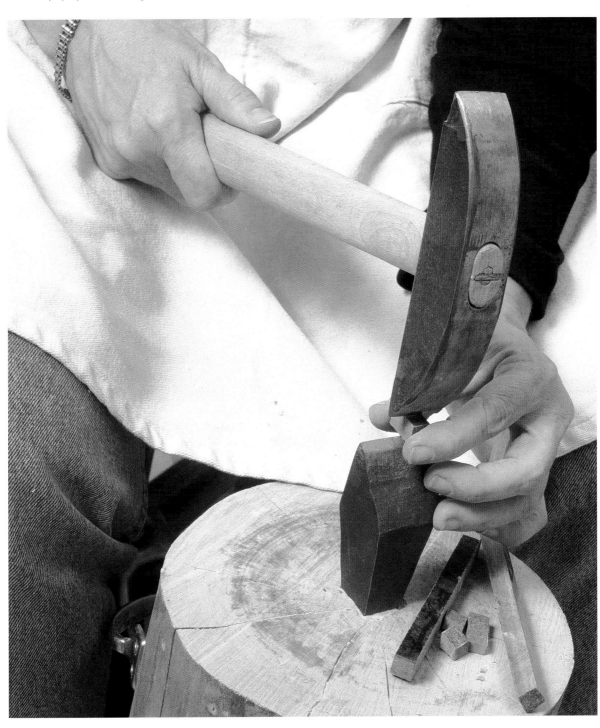

lose its appeal as an area gets a little odd from using leftovers. Always be sure to leave some tiles whole for cutting into slightly larger than average tesserae. How small you cut is a personal decision. Just be aware that extremely small tesserae will mean a lot of grout lines. The important thing about creating tesserae is to figure out what works for you. There is no right or wrong to mosaics; it's a very individual art. Eventually, nipping tesserae becomes therapeutic and quite soothing. Many mosaic artists develop an almost Zen-like ability to "think" the cuts into happening.

PLACING THE TESSERAE

There are several ways to adhere tesserae to the surface. Some mosaicists prefer to "butter" the adhesive on the back of each tessera and then press it down. I apply the adhesive to a small area of the surface and then press the pieces into it. No matter which technique is used, it's important to control the thickness of the adhesive. You should apply enough adhesive to hold each piece firmly. Too much, however, will not give the grout enough room to anchor in the joints between the tiles. If a project is going to be grouted, the adhesive shouldn't be more than half the thickness of the tile. An ungrouted project offers more flexibility in the application of the tesserae. For example, if you are working with cement-based adhesive, the tesserae might have deep grooves between them to emphasize the texture. Alternatively, you can spread a thicker coat of the thinset and then press each piece deep enough so that it virtually "self-grouts" the project.

When actually placing the tesserae, press firmly and give each piece a little twist while seating it against the backing surface. This creates a little suction that really "anchors" the piece.

The most valuable advice that I can give you about placing tesserae is to learn to think two or three pieces ahead. If you find yourself fussing with a piece that you can't get right, it's probably not the one creating the difficulty. Look back two or three pieces and you'll usually find the culprit. Small oddities will ripple forward through a mosaic. A piece that is only slightly off can create an obvious awkwardness further down the line. Given all that, if you can't get a certain piece to cut right, don't be too concerned. When the mosaic is finished you'll have a hard time finding it again.

If I come to a spot where I'm not sure about the best way to lay something, I put it down the first way and take a good look at it. Then I'll lay some alternative pieces on top of the first ones and try it that way. Working back and forth between the two usually makes the decision obvious. This technique is especially helpful when blending or "feathering" colors into one another. Try it several ways to avoid the polka dot look. Successfully feathering or mixing several colors sets up a flickery, almost vibrating effect that adds depth.

When possible, use a turntable or Lazy Susan under your mosaic while you are working. This allows you to easily work from other sides. In addition, since you're not leaning over as much while you're working, it saves wear and tear on your back.

Before I stop working, I use a dental pick or pointy tool to clean any excess adhesive that has oozed out from under the tiles. Letting it dry as is will make it difficult to place the neighboring tesserae when you begin working again. Keep a 2-inch (5-cm) paintbrush handy to clear your working surface of shards.

GROUT LINES

Whether the mosaic is grouted or ungrouted, the spaces between the tesserae (called interstices or grout lines) offer another opportunity to control the rhythm of a mosaic. The mind's eye looks at all

> **Tip:** *Some people like to lay out a section of mosaic and adjust the placement before actually gluing the pieces down. Invariably, the tesserae don't fit together again in exactly the same way. If you like to work this way, try using tweezers and move only a few pieces at a time.*

KEYSTONING

Keystoning is an important technique to understand when laying tiles along a curve. If square tesserae are laid around a curve, the corners will meet on the inside curve and gap on the outside, leaving a v-shape space between the pieces. This happens because the outside of the curve is bigger than the inside. Cutting the tesserae into "keystone" shapes will make the spaces between the tiles consistent and allow the eye to smoothly read across the curve. This means an angle is cut off the tile along the whole side. The degree of angle cut depends on the tightness of the curve. The tighter the curve, the sharper the angle.

The biggest issue with keystoning is understanding how sharp to cut the angle. Look at each curve as being part of a circle. Find the center of that circle and imagine a line along the edge of the tile to the center. That's the angle that needs to be cut. If the angle is too sharp, the next piece will have to be cut with an opposing angle to keep the spacing consistent. This means the first cut was wrong, which throws the rhythm of the circle off.

If you are working around a difficult spot, make smaller, subtler cuts to several tesserae. This fools the eye by not calling attention to a single dramatic angle.

It is worth the effort to learn how to keystone. A curve that is well laid moves the eye along it and enhances the design. Like anything else, the first time is hard but after working with the shapes and fitting them together, it becomes easier. It also helps educate your eye to the best way of fitting pieces together.

3-29 Keystoning.

the small pieces in a mosaic and makes sense out of them as a whole. Consistent spacing contributes to this assimilation. Inconsistent spacing adds tension and a helter-skelter feeling to a piece. Interesting effects can be obtained by changing the spacing between different areas. For example, a tightly spaced foreground will "pop out" from a looser spaced background.

The more you work with tesserae and shapes, fitting them together, the more possibilities you will see. The actual process of laying a mosaic has its own kind of rhythm that is reflected in the mosaic. When working a background, be sure the laying is consistent as it moves behind the foreground. This continuity from one side to the other helps the eye "read" a mosaic.

An unintended grout "river" is an easy mistake to make when laying a mosaic. Many times you don't even notice it until the piece is grouted and it's too late to fix it. A grout river is formed when the joints between the tiles line up and create a line that may be counter to the design (Photo 3–30). A grout river can cause a mosaic to visually "break apart." The design appears to crack. The best thing to do is to just stay aware of the unintended patterns that may appear as you are working. Grout rivers can be used intentionally to emphasize a design feature. The trick is to make them work for you.

PREPARING THE BASE

Properly preparing the base for a mosaic is an important first step toward creating a lasting work of art. Most surfaces require minimum preparation, and the goal is the same for all of them: a clean, dust-free surface with adequate "tooth" for good adhesion.

Wood surfaces should be sealed. Although it won't keep the wood from rotting or warping, sealing will prevent the wood from absorbing moisture

3-30 *Opus palladianum*, or crazy paving, with a horizontal grout river.

from the adhesive or grout and thus, prevent proper curing. Otherwise, the curing process shortens, which can result in cracks. I seal wood surfaces with a mixture of one-part PVA, or WeldBond, and four- to five-parts water. Just paint it on quickly and cover all the sides. For example, if you're using a board, make sure you cover the top, bottom, and four edges. Allow 30 minutes for the sealer to dry, then the base is ready to mosaic. If the wood has an especially smooth surface, like MDF, use a nail or screwdriver to scratch up the surface for added "tooth" or texture before sealing. If the wood has been painted, make sure it's not flaky or loose. Sand the surface to add a little texture, if necessary. You can also clean furniture with rubbing alcohol to remove any oils or furniture polish.

Cement backer board or statuary only needs to be clean and dust-free before starting. If the cement has been painted, it may need to be sanded or sand-blasted before mosaicking.

Pottery and terra-cotta should be sealed with the same PVA and water mixture as used for wood surfaces. Although this doesn't really "seal" the surface, it makes the surface a little sticky so that the tesserae will stay during application. It also allows the grout to cure properly. Once the grout has cured, use a penetrating grout sealer on the interior and exterior of the pot. This is very important. Otherwise, the pottery will absorb the moisture from its interior, which may seep through to the adhesive and cause mildew and darkening.

Tip: *Don't use waterproofing sealers that are manufactured for outside decks. These water repellents will repel the adhesive. The tesserae will stick for a while, but ultimately the mosaic may peel off in big sections.*

ADHESIVES

Many glues and adhesives are available in tubes and caulking containers. Read all the directions and warning labels before using them. Many of these are perfect for certain uses but can be very toxic to breathe or get on your skin. Follow the recommended safety precautions.

Some commonsense guidelines apply when working with all adhesives. Remember to leave room in the tile joints if you're planning on grouting. Also, it's easier to avoid getting adhesive on the top of the tiles than it is to clean the adhesive off them. Finally, be sure that each piece is anchored securely by the adhesive.

PVA

PVA, or WeldBond, glue is easy to use, odorless, and dries clearly. Buy a small bottle with a nozzle applicator. A small bottle is easier to handle and can be refilled many times. You can apply the glue to the base and place several tesserae at a time, or apply the glue to the back of each piece and then press it onto the base. Clean up any glue that squishes out from beneath the tile to where another piece will be placed later. Otherwise, the surface becomes bumpy. Be sure and leave room for grouting.

When working on a three-dimensional surface, refrigerate the PVA before using. This thickens the glue and helps prevent pieces from sliding. You can also prevent sliding by allowing the glue to air dry a few minutes before applying the tesserae.

CEMENT-BASED ADHESIVE

Mixing cement-based adhesive (or thinset mortar) with liquid latex admixture improves its strength, adhesion, and weather resistance. To ensure compatibility, use the cement-based adhesive and liquid latex admixture from the same manufacturer

(Photo 3–31). Follow the directions for mixing.

Some mortars contain powdered admixture and only need to be mixed with water. Always wear a dust mask or respirator when handling the powder. Mix the cement-based adhesive in a disposable cup to the consistency of a thick paste or cake frosting. Make it a little thicker if you are applying it to a vertical surface. This will prevent the tesserae from sliding. Use a palette knife to spread the cement-based adhesive over a small area at a time to prevent it from "skinning up." Keep the mix covered when you're not using it. It will still be good for several hours. When the cement-based adhesive ceases being sticky, throw the container away and mix up a new batch. Don't try to put in more admix and don't try to save any you may have left overnight. The bond will not be strong and, besides, thinset is relatively inexpensive.

It requires some experience to judge how thick to apply thinset. If grouting, limit the depth to no more than half the height of the tile. This leaves plenty of room in the joints for the grout.

With practice, you can use thinset to "self-grout" the mosaic. Control both the thickness of the mortar and the push in of each tessera for the textural effect desired. As a piece is pressed into the adhesive, give it a little twist to really anchor it.

Unlike glue, cement-based adhesive has "memory." With glue, you can move a tessera slightly and the glue will seep into the empty space. But if the thinset mortar has begun to set up, even slightly, then moving a piece will require fresh thinset. The cement "remembers" the first position and will not make a firm bond.

3-31 Mixing cement-based adhesive with admix.

Cement colorants, or powdered or universal pigments, can be used to modify the color of the thinset. Do some experiments first to be sure of the result.

TILE MASTIC

Tile mastic is thick and very sticky. It can be buttered on the base or applied to the back of each tessera. Mastic is especially good for working on vertical or three-dimensional pieces, because the pieces won't slide. It can be messy to work with because it sticks to you too, so use a craft stick to apply the mastic and keep paper towels handy (Photo 3–32). Remember to only use it indoors on projects with limited exposure to water.

GROUTING

Grouting can enhance a mosaic and pull it all together, or it can be a big disappointment. Check out the grout study in Photo 3–33 and see what a difference grout can make. The same color tiles are in the exact same places. The only difference is the choice of grout color. If the tesserae are all of a medium tone, gray tends to blend the colors, black intensifies them while white fractures them apart. Different combinations of tesserae will react differently. (Detailed grouting instructions are on pages 112–115.)

Choosing a Color

The safest way to choose the correct grout color is to do a test on a few tiles. Just glue eight to ten tesserae several times on a sample and try out your colors. Many times the choice is clear. But if you still aren't sure, choosing natural gray grout is rarely a mistake. There's something about a medium gray grout that makes it disappear to the eye. It seems to just drop into the background.

White grout is seldom the best color to use in a mosaic. It can be very severe. It tends to break a piece up and can emphasize any mistakes made in laying. The exceptions to using white are for broken china mosaics and a mosaic where white is the main color. Choosing a color that is the same as the major elements will blend them together and occasionally lose some of the detail. If a mosaic has both

light and dark areas then use a color that is in between. This makes the "fracturing" effect even across the mosaic. Be careful with intense-color grouts. They may overpower a mosaic.

Whenever possible, use a pre-blended color of grout. If you can't find a color you like, you can custom mix colors, but make note of the exact proportions. If mixing dry components, keep a container of the custom mix for potential repairs. Make sure custom colors are thoroughly mixed. It's difficult to tell the color variations when the grout is wet, but they will show up after drying. Pure pigments or universal colorants give the strongest grout colors. The pigments come in a powdered or liquid form. If you're using the liquid, substitute some of the water with pigment or colorant when mixing. For an even stronger color, mix up the grout as usual and apply it. Then, while wearing gloves, rub the liquid pigment into the wet grout for the desired effect. Be ready to clean the pigment off the tiles quickly.

> **Tip:** *When blending a custom mix of dry grout, set aside a small amount of the dry mix. If you add too much water to the grout when mixing, then you will have the right blend on hand for correcting the consistency.*

Acrylic paint is not the best choice for coloring grout. It is a latex-based paint rather than a pigment. Adding enough to affect a color change will cause the grout to have a plastic-looking surface. Too much acrylic paint may also cause the grout to crack.

Mixing

Use a sanded grout that already has polymers added for enhanced strength. If this isn't available, you can use liquid admix instead of water. The goal is to get a consistency that is similar to thick cookie dough. It is difficult to give the exact proportions of grout to water. Both the brand and the humidity can cause this to vary.

It's easy to suddenly have a grout that's too wet.

3–32 Apply mastic with a craft stick.

3–33 Grout study: each tile is the same color in the same place with different grouts.

To avoid this, as the mix gets close to the correct consistency, add a little water at a time. If it gets too wet, add a little powder to bring it back to the right texture. Grout that is too wet is difficult to clean and prone to having air bubbles. It may also crack as it dries. Working with a grout that is a little thick has two advantages. First, there will be fewer air bubbles, and you can clean it faster and easier, thereby avoiding grout haze.

After mixing, set the grout aside to "slake" for 10 minutes before using. Then restir and apply. This allows the chemical process to begin and then breaks it back down. The second hardening creates a stronger grout. Once the grout has slaked, don't add more water or powder. Retempering will weaken the grout.

CLEANING UP

Spoon all the leftover grout onto the small pile of newspapers you grouted on. Fold up all but the bottom piece of newspaper and throw it away. Wad up the last piece of newspaper, stand over a trashcan, and dry rub the grout bowl. This pulls the moisture out of any remaining grout and turns it back to sand. Cleanup is easy now. Take your bucket, bowl, and tools outside. Use a hose to clean everything up. Do not clean up in the sink. Grout and cement will quickly plug up a drain.

GROUT HAZE

Occasionally, a mosaic will develop a foggy film known as grout haze. It appears to clean off with water but comes back when the mosaic dries. It is usually caused by leaving the grout on the surface of the tiles for too long. This is most likely to happen when a mosaic is very textured and hard to clean. Wait a week for the grout to cure before applying an acid wash.

First, try cleaning the mosaic with white vinegar. The mild acidity of the vinegar will usually do the trick. If that doesn't work, use an acid tile cleaner. Wear rubber gloves and an apron when you do this. Follow the manufacturer's instructions for mixing and using the cleaner. These are the basic steps: Mix a small amount of cleaner with the appropriate amount of water. Have a bowl of clean water and several sponges. Place the mosaic over a thick stack of newspaper. Wet the mosaic surface with a spongeful of clean water. Use a different sponge to apply the cleaner. It will begin to slightly bubble. You can use the sponge to scrub the surface a little. Don't use a brush or press vigorously, as you can easily dig out the grout with the acid. After a minute or two, squeeze clean water over the mosaic. The water will stop the chemical process. Lift the mosaic to drain the water off, then set it aside to dry.

Even if a mosaic doesn't have grout haze, you may still want to give it a vinegar wash. It will brighten the mosaic.

Before Grouting

Some bases, such as picture frames and trays, require masking off areas that you don't want exposed to grout. After you apply the grout, remove the tape while the grout is still wet. Simply pull back flatly against the tape and away from the mosaic. Then smooth out any rough edges with your gloved finger.

FINAL STEPS

Any mosaic that is going to be outdoors or subject to staining should be sealed with a penetrating grout sealer. Do this after the grout has cured. Periodic resealing will extend the life of an outdoor mosaic.

There are lots of ways to finish and hang a mosaic. For flat mosaics, it's tempting to put tiles along the edge, but this is asking for trouble. Edges are prone to getting bumped and the tiles may pop off. Repairing it would involve gluing and regrouting the edge. If you still decide to do the edge in tile, do the sides first and then the top can overlap slightly. This prevents the edges of the tiles from creating a distracting outline around the mosaic. Some people also try spreading grout on the edge, but it will ultimately pop off. You can use thinset cement to add an edge to a piece, if you like an earthy look. For tables, use a base with a raised rim. Alternative edges are copper or metal stripping.

Many mosaicists frame their wall pieces in a narrow metal or wood frame. Since a mosaic already has a lot going on, choose a plain frame. D-ring mirror hangers are good for hanging mosaics (Photo 3–34). Be sure and use the correct size for the weight of the mosaic. Two hangers on the back will distribute the weight safely. Make sure the screws aren't thicker than the base. Adding a little glue under the hanger will make it even more secure.

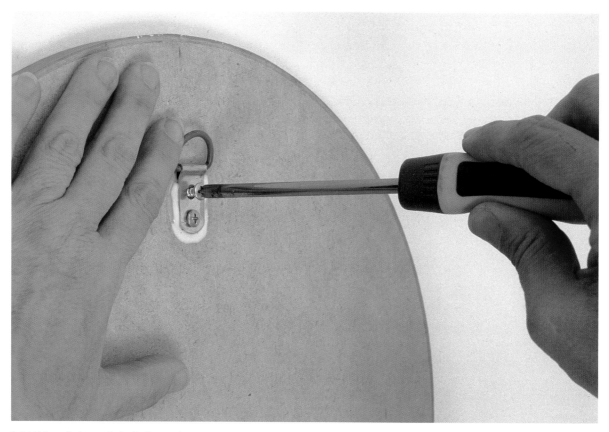

3–34 Fixing a D-ring on the back of a mosaic.

DESIGNING A MOSAIC

CHAPTER

Designing a mosaic can be as simple as recycling a broken plate onto a trivet or as complicated as planning a community mosaic. Any mosaic project requires both practical and artistic decisions. The practical issues are specific to the art of mosaics while the artistic questions may be as general as composition and balance. This chapter covers both the artistic decisions that are distinct to a mosaic as well as the practical considerations that go into its creation.

Planning a mosaic begins with choosing a subject. It may be abstract or representational. Don't be daunted by the design process, as a mosaic can be pleasing by virtue of its fascinating surface texture alone. Ideas for a mosaic can come from anywhere: a museum visit, a tour of Europe, clip art, or even the way light plays across water. Certain images and themes catch the mind's eye repeatedly. Pay attention to the images, textures, and colors that are personally captivating. Those affinities will show up in your finished mosaic.

No matter what the source of inspiration, there are ways to make the development of an idea easier. Understanding the artistic implications of design decisions will become second nature with experience. Acquiring knowledge about the components of a mosaic and how the different parts interact will speed up the process. Many of your decisions will become obvious after considering the practical requirements of the mosaic.

For those who are starting out, this chapter may make creating a

Above: **Jane Muir.** *Marine Roundel*, 2000. 21-inch (53-cm) diameter. Vitreous glass, smalti, golds, glass fusions. Photo by the artist.

mosaic appear complicated. The checklist at the end of the chapter will help you keep it straight. Begin with a small project and use limited materials to become familiar with the process of fitting shapes into a mosaic. As you gain experience, your instinct and personal style will make many decisions automatic. In the process, you may become hooked.

ARTISTIC CONSIDERATIONS

Taking advantage of a mosaic's inherent features will improve any design. First and most important are the tesserae. When the human eye sees a mosaic, an interesting thing happens. The mind's eye looks at all those small pieces, makes sense out of them as a whole, and assimilates the image in the viewer's mind. You should adapt an image for a mosaic by emphasizing the elements that strengthen the design while simplifying, or eliminating, those that confuse the eye. A stylized approach gives the mosaic a contemporary feel that enhances it.

The master mosaicists of old had two distinct work advantages: the size and distance of their mosaic. Since they were able to work on a huge scale, they could fit a lot of details into their large floor, wall, and ceiling mosaics. At a distance, a mosaic on a high ceiling, for example, made it easier for the eye to assimilate all those little pieces into an integrated, coherent whole. In addition, the most successful and engaging mosaics had a freshness and immediacy to the design. There was an acceptance of the materials' limitations.

Contemporary mosaic artists don't always have

4–1 Above: **Elaine M. Goodwin.** *Song of Light,* 1999. 20 x 15 inches (51 x 38 cm). Marble, smalti, golds, and fool's gold. Photo by John Melville.

4–2 Below: **Tessa Hunkin.** *Food,* 1998. 2 x 6 feet (60 cm x 1.8 m). Vitreous glass. Photo by June Black.

4–3 Opposite Page: **Maggy Howarth.** *Zodiac Garden,* 1996. 26 x 26 feet (8 x 8 m). Pebbles. Photo by Johnathan Hill.

the benefit of large walls and ceilings. The lesson, then, is to simplify. When developing an intricate design, think about ways to keep the look and feel while eliminating the complexity. For example, if your mosaic design contains foliage, then five well-done leaves will give you a better result than forcing in ten leaves. The eye will understand the "leafiness" of the design and make better sense of it as a whole. If the leaves have stems to a branch, then create three stems and allow the mind's eye to understand that all the leaves are connected. Defining each and every stem reduces the area to many little lines and a lot of grout.

Develop a sense of what's necessary for the

Tip: *A trip to the copier shop will help enlarge a design to the correct size for a project. Use carbon or transfer paper to get the design onto the backing surface. If you are drawing freehand, use chalk. When the design is right, use a marker to make it permanent.*

design and what is too much. The goal is to recreate the essence of the image. Don't be afraid to simplify the design. The inherent appeal of a mosaic

COMMON MISTAKES

- Tesserae that are out of scale to the majority of pieces may affect the strength of your design. For example, putting small pieces on the edge of a mosaic will tend to pull the eye toward the side. Or placing just one or two odd-shaped, or very small pieces, in the middle can make the mind's eye sense that something is slightly off. If an inconsistency in size is necessary, make that oddness consistent across the mosaic by placing those odd pieces in several places.

- Triangle shapes can also be problematical. Be careful of placing triangular tesserae with all the small points coming together. This creates star-shaped patterns that will be even more evident after grouting. Little oddities like these can throw off the rhythm of a mosaic.

- There will often be a few places where a grout line is a little wider than normal but only a small sliver or triangle will fit in. Avoid the impulse to fill these spots. Small slivers call attention to the problem while a slightly wider space filled with grout will tend to disappear. Again, "consistent inconsistencies" will really help. Just make sure there are a few spots across the mosaic that are a little wider.

---

surface will compensate for it.

Good composition is important in any work of art. The actual design drawing for a mosaic is called a cartoon. The cartoon is a full-size sketch that serves as a guide to the creation. If you're uncomfortable with drawing and designing, find a picture you like, simplify it, and use a copier to enlarge the sketch to the desired size. Then use carbon paper to transfer it to your base.

Although it is not a precise diagram, the cartoon should show the major elements of the mosaic as well as the intended flow of the tesserae. The

unique appeal of a mosaic is created by its materials and their placement. If you use alternative materials and placement, the same cartoon can yield a different mosaic.

Many mosaic artists work with only the sketchiest of cartoons and find the details as the creation progresses. Let the materials drive the project. The serendipity of a tile breaking a certain way or a surprisingly crystalline piece of marble can add freshness and spontaneity to a mosaic. It is the mosaicist's job to recognize and take advantage of these happy accidents. Planning a project down to the last detail will result in a technically pleasing mosaic, but it may miss the essence of mosaic art.

LAYING THE TESSERAE

Mosaic is all about flow and pattern. Even in a crazy paving design there are underlying principles that contribute to the work's success. Studying the mosaics of the past and the techniques that have endured for centuries is very worthwhile for contemporary mosaicists Understanding how a mosaic works and the techniques that achieve a certain look can have a direct bearing on even the most random creations.

Tip: *Here's an old art school trick that's very useful for mosaicists. When creating a mosaic, occasionally step away from the worktable and look at the project with squinted eyes. This reduces the amount of detail and allows you to see possible design flaws and imbalances. In addition, it reveals a better sense of the tonal relationships between colors. The color changes may be too subtle and more contrast may be needed, or vice versa.*

4–4 Opus regulatum. Photo by author. 　*4–5 Opus tessellatum.* Photo by author. 　*4–6 Opus vermiculatum.* Photo by author.

There are two aspects to how tesserae are laid: *andamento* and *opus*. *Andamento* is Italian for trend or course. How one "courses" the tesserae can determine the rhythm and flow of a piece. Varying the widths of the rows and the spacing between create a sense of movement. The work of a mosaicist with a strong *andamento* can often be identified by its distinctive rhythm.

While the rhythm is determined by the *andamento*, the pattern, or lack thereof, is determined by the *opus*. *Opus* is the Latin word for a creative work,

meaning the way in which a mosaic is worked. The most common ways of working a mosaic are explained here.

Opus regulatum (Photo 4–4) looks exactly like it sounds: regular. Tesserae are laid in a pattern like a grid or graph paper. Both the vertical and horizontal grout lines are aligned. Tile comes this way when it is shipped on sheets. *Regulatum* is useful in creating geometric patterns or for a background (Photo 4–8). Since *regulatum* can be a little predictable, it is possible to lose the interest and texture of the mosaic.

4–7 Above Left: An example of an *opus tessellatum* background combined with *opus vermiculatum*. **Black and White Floor**, first century C.E. Vatican Museum, Rome. Photo by George Fishman.

4–8 Above Right: An example of *opus regulatum*. **Eliana Raposo.** *Stone Carpet*, 2000. Marble. Photo by Luis Gomes.

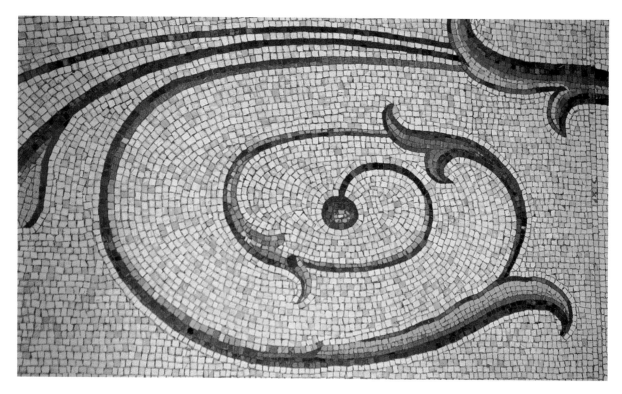

4–9 *Top: Opus vermiculatum*, second century c.e. Vatican Museum, Rome. Photo by author.

4–10 *Above Left: Opus palladianum* or crazy paving. Photo by author.

4–11 *Above Right:* An example of *opus palladianum*. **Antoni Gaudí** and **Josep M. Jujol**. *Fountain*, 1905–1914. Parc Güell, Barcelona, Spain. Photo by author.

Opus tessellatum (Photo 4–5) is similar to *regulatum* but with more interest. *Tessellatum* is like a brick-laying pattern. The horizontal grout lines are aligned while the vertical lines are offset. *Tessellatum* is often used as a contrast to a flowing or intricate

foreground (Photo 4–7). The regularity serves to emphasize the foreground.

Opus vermiculatum (Photo 4–6) is laying tesserae in a worm-like, winding manner. It is a very expressive way of working the tesserae and gives the mosaic a sense of movement. *Vermiculatum* can be effective in both representational and abstract designs. For example, *opus vermiculatum* is the perfect choice for laying tesserae when creating hair. It is also especially useful for filling in areas between unusual-shaped objects (Photo 4–9). Movement and motion will be

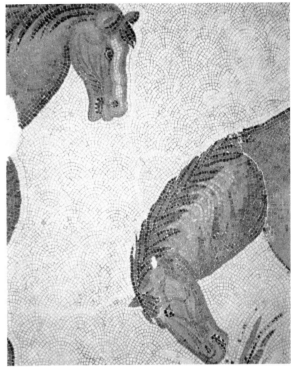

enhanced if it is carried out in multiple rows, like a radiating halo. If *vermiculatum* is used over the entire surface of a mosaic, it becomes extremely expressive and may be called *opus musivum*. *Musivum* was traditionally used over a large area, such as a wall or ceiling, to add drama and energy.

Combining *opus tessellatum* and *opus vermiculatum* is a technique the Romans used to great advantage. An image is outlined with a single or double row of background-colored tesserae. The rest of the background is then worked in *opus tessellatum*. The outline serves to anchor the image to the background. While it sounds a little obvious, in practice, it's a very effective technique. Look at pictures of Roman mosaics combining *tessellatum* and *vermiculatum* (Photo 4–7) and it's surprising how subtle it can be.

4–12 Top Left: An example of *opus sectile*. **Julie Richey** and **Laura Larsen.** *Daphne*, 1992. 40 x 40 inches (102 x 102 cm). Marble. Photo by the artist.

4–13 Top Right: Two horses in an *opus circumactum* background, fourth century c.e. The Great Palace, Istanbul, Turkey. Photo by author.

4–14 Above Left: **Opus circumactum.** Photo by author.

4–15 Above Right: **Cosmati Work Floor.** San Marco, Venice. Photo by George Fishman.

4–16 **Black and White Floor,** first century c.e. Russi, Italy. Photo by author.

Opus palladianum (Photo 4–10), or crazy paving, is laying random-shaped tesserae in a random manner. It is extremely popular in contemporary mosaics (Photo 4–11). It can add both tension and energy to a design. Crazy paving with broken

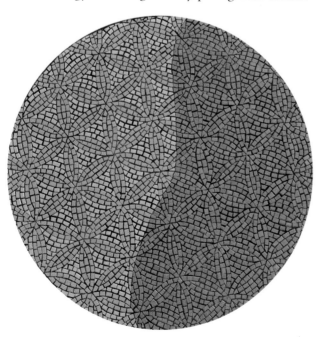

4–17 **Lia Catalano.** *Fractured,* 2001. 24-inch (61-cm) diameter. Unglazed ceramic. Photo by the artist.

china is called *picassiette*. Beginners will find it easy to create an appealing mosaic using random tesserae, but the skill involved in doing *opus palladianum* shouldn't be underestimated.

Some mosaics utilize larger pieces of a single material to define an element of the mosaic. This is called *opus sectile*. An example of this are the Cosmati floors in many Italian churches (Photo 4–15). These abstract floors are created from marble sections fitted tightly together. Many of the same churches have cloisters surrounded by columns decorated with Cosmati insets in glass, marble, and gold. Another form of *opus sectile* is seen in hard stone mosaics, or *pietra dura*. The pictorial scenes are created from colored marble and stones fitted tightly together (Photo 4–12). For example, a blue-veined marble might be used to create the sky. Today, stained glass is often worked in *opus sectile*.

One of the loveliest backgrounds created by the Romans is called *opus circumactum* Photo 4–14. It is a fan-shaped pattern repeated over and over. It looks difficult, but once the pattern, spacing, and interrelationships are understood, the work moves quickly (Photo 4–13).

4–18 A tile color wheel with hot colors (red, orange, yellow) and cool colors (green, blue, purple). Photo by Sheila Cunningham.

COLOR AND SPACE

Mosaic is an artistic medium with finite options. Colors can't be blended like paint. When choosing the colors for a mosaic, you should always examine the tesserae in natural daylight, as artificial lighting can mask the true relationships between colors. A common mistake is to choose colors that are too subtle in contrast. The size of the final mosaic will also have an impact on your color choices. A small project doesn't have room for understated color changes. The choice of grout may also even out and blend colors, which compounds the mistake. It's always a good idea to lay out several tiles in the selected colors and confirm the relationships between them. Some colors will appear to be good choices when looked at individually, but this may change when they are placed next to one another. For example, contrasting colors will intensify one another. Also, setting tesserae closer together may change their color value (their relative lightness or darkness) and affect the balance of a mosaic.

The actual placement of the tesserae also has an impact. A mosaic is all about positive and negative space. The tesserae are positive and the spaces (or interstices) in between are the negatives. In addition to the *opera* (plural for *opus*) techniques mentioned, there are many ways to enhance the eye's

assimilation. Changing the patterns of laying can push certain areas toward to the eye and cause others to recede. Contrasting matte finish tesserae with shiny ones offers added interest to the surface. Changing the size, or scale, of the tesserae and varying the spacing introduces movement and tension. In addition, you can tilt a tessera to catch the light or even set it on edge to change the texture. Experiment with different methods of laying and learn the effects of using the tesserae in alternative ways. It will add freshness and variety to your mosaic.

With regard to the negative space of a mosaic, you should keep in mind that in many ways the grout lines and spaces are just as important. Thinking about a mosaic in these terms offers a different perspective on the design as well as opportunities for creativity. As mentioned in the "Techniques" chapter (see pages 92–93), it isn't unusual, especially in the beginning, to grout a piece and find unexpected patterns or "rivers" in the grout lines. Understanding the negative spaces not only eliminates a lot of surprises when grouting, but it also offers opportunities for enhancing a design. Grout rivers can also be a great tool for adding dimension and form to an image. In addition, varying the width of these spaces adds *andamento*, or flow, to a mosaic. Consistent grout spacing is pleasing to the eye and makes a mosaic easier to "read" while inconsistent grout lines can add tension. The choice of color can also make or break the project. If in doubt, avoid surprises by doing a grout study (see page 96).

The decision of whether or not to grout offers even more design options. If a mosaic is to be used as a floor or tabletop, then grouting is required to maintain a flat surface that is free of dirt and debris. Artistic mosaics, however, are often left ungrouted. This offers expanded opportunities for texture and surface features because the interstices take on added importance.

PRACTICAL CONSIDERATIONS

When planning a mosaic, it is important to consider all the practical issues. Ask yourself: Will the mosaic be indoors or out? Will it be subject to freeze and thaw cycles? Is the location of where it will be dry, somewhat humid, or even underwater? What will be the lighting conditions? Will there be bright lighting or will it be a little dark? Will the mosaic be exposed to direct or indirect sunlight? Will there even be a glare? Will the mosaic be a fine art or decorative piece? The answers will determine what materials, adhesives, and techniques are needed for the mosaic.

If a mosaic will be outdoors, the choice of bases and adhesives to use narrows significantly. It takes considerable effort to create a mosaic. It would be a shame if the base or adhesive disintegrated over time. Since wood will eventually rot, it is a poor choice for an exterior substrate. Certain glues are sensitive to water, so they're not an option as well. You need to carefully consider using metal if your mosaic will be subject to freezing and thawing. The metal will expand and contract. In similar cases, using a material like bathroom wall tiles with a chalky back may result in the glaze popping off in a hard freeze. These issues need to be worked out one by one to ensure that the mosaic is created from the best materials for its purpose.

The lighting conditions also have an impact on the materials chosen for a project. If there is a great deal of glare, then using mirror will become a problem. However, in indirect lighting, mirror can catch the eye and create interest. In an area with less light, subtle color changes may blend and lose their intensity. Setting the tesserae at slight angles will take advantage of the existing light. Darker locations will make the choice of grout color more important, as it can add definition that

is lost by the poor lighting conditions. Halogen lighting will often create "hot spots" on glazed tile. When seen at an angle, the play of light over a vitreous glass surface is often an unexpected pleasure. The actual image may become lost, but the texture and intricacy of the surface is still beautiful. Practice looking at mosaics under different lighting conditions and you'll learn the various effects.

Whether the mosaic is intended to be a fine art or a decorative art and craft piece also affects the artist's choice of materials. A mosaic can be an interesting balance between the two, but with a fine-art mosaic you have more options. A decorative mosaic, on the other hand, needs to be functional, so the choice of materials is more constrained. For example, a tabletop requires tesserae that are flat so that drinking glasses don't tip over. For a floor or shower wall, you should avoid using smalti because of their sharp and uneven edges. Vitreous glass isn't recommended for high-traffic floor areas.

Finally, whether the mosaic will be grouted is another question that has bearing on your choice of materials. Try and think of the possible results from the materials you pick. And even if the finished mosaic doesn't turn out right, it will be a valuable learning experience.

DESIGN DECISION CHECKLIST
A mosaic design is the culmination of many decisions and the artist's experiences. This checklist will serve as a reminder of the relevant issues to consider in approaching a design. Not all the items will apply to every mosaic.

ARTISTIC	PRACTICAL	STEPS
Simplify	Indoor/outdoor	Choose an image
Scale	Water exposure	Adapt a design
Opus (or not)	Lighting	Choose the manner of laying
Tesserae	Purpose	Choose the materials
Positive and negative space	Grout	Choose the spacing

4–19 **Jerry Carter.** *Second Genesis* (detail), 1984–1985. Smalti, porcelain. Note the intricate working of the smalti. Parco del Pace, Ravenna, Italy. Photo by author.

CREATING A MOSAIC

CHAPTER

There are two primary techniques in creating a mosaic: the direct method and the indirect (or reverse) method. Each has advantages and difficulties, so it's important to think about a project's practical requirements when choosing a method. This chapter will show you each method by creating a mosaic. The direct method project also includes detailed, step-by-step instructions for grouting. Variations of these two techniques, such as the double reverse method and working with mesh, are also covered.

THE DIRECT METHOD

The direct method is the most common and easiest method of mosaicking. The tesserae are pressed directly onto the base using adhesive. Mosaics made in this method may be grouted or ungrouted, depending on the desired look and the purpose of the mosaic. Working directly also offers the opportunity to create a mosaic with varying textures. A flat surface, like a tabletop, can be achieved as long as materials of the same thickness are used and the adhesive is applied evenly. The direct method allows you to see how a mosaic is going to look as it is being created.

Three-dimensional surfaces are usually worked directly, although it is a little trickier. If the mosaic's curves are sharp, you will need to use smaller pieces to conform to the shape. Use a thick adhesive, like thinset or mastic, to prevent the tesserae from slipping. It is also a good idea to use a box or support to place the mosaic on its side. This allows you to keep the working surface horizontal.

HOUSE NUMBER
(DIRECT METHOD)
LEVEL: EASY

MATERIALS
- One 6 x 12-inch (15 x 30-cm) floor tile
- 1-inch (2.5-cm) matte ceramic frost-proof tiles in rust, beige, brown, and two shades of green
- Brown sanded grout
- PVA glue (WeldBond)
- Penetrating grout sealer

TOOLS
- Side biter nippers
- Spatula
- Dental pick
- Rubber squeegee
- Grout sponge
- Water bucket
- Safety glasses
- Rubber gloves
- Paper towels

Prepare the Base

1. Use the rough back of the 6 x 12-inch floor tile, as it will bond better than the glazed front. Transfer the design onto the tile with carbon paper and then trace over the lines with a permanent marker (Photos 5–1 and 5–2).

5–1 Use carbon paper to transfer the design to the back of the large tile.

5–2 Darken the design with a permanent marker.

Numbers and Leaves

2. Put on safety glasses. Use the nippers to shape the green tiles into leaves. Lay the tiles down with some space in between so that the spaces resemble the veins of the leaves. Cut the beige tiles into quarters for the numbers. Glue the tesserae to the tile base using PVA glue (Photo 5–3). Use enough glue to firmly anchor the piece, but be careful to keep the joints clear for grouting. Note the shape of the bottom tiles in the zero (Photo 5–4). This is a good example of keystoning a smooth curve.

5–3 Apply the tesserae for the leaves and numbers using PVA glue.

5–4 Keystoning the 0 makes the curve smooth.

Background

3. I've chosen to lay the background in *opus regulatum,* or grid pattern. The predictable evenness of this pattern helps push the numbers forward. Start on one side and work across to the other. When you're a few inches away from the end, lay a few tesserae out along the top to check if any spacing adjustments are necessary. Use the dental pick to clean off any excess adhesive (Photos 5–5 and 5–6). Leave about ⅛ inch (3 mm) on all the edges. This allows you to bevel the grout to the edge. Dry overnight before grouting.

Grout Test

4. On this project, I decided to do a small grout test before choosing the color. I took a scrap tile

and glued three sets of the colors in the project. I grouted each set differently: tan, brown, and gray (Photo 5–7). After allowing the grout to dry back to it's natural color, I chose the brown grout because it intensifies the contrast between the colors.

5–5 Clean the excess glue from the joints.

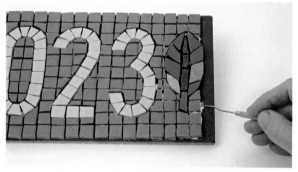

5–6 And clean excess glue from beside the tiles.

Grouting

5. The amount of grout you need to mix depends on the spacing between the tesserae and the depth of the tiles. It's always better to mix too much rather than too little. Add water to the powder a little at a time. Be careful not to spill any grout down the sink drain. Always stir to the bottom,

5–7 Deciding on the grout color using the grout study.

turning up any pockets of dry grout. Continue adding water and mixing thoroughly until the grout resembles a thick cookie dough (Photo 5–8).

6. Allow the grout to "slake" or sit for 10 minutes. In the meantime, fill your bucket with water for cleaning and prepare the grout area by spreading out a pile of unfolded newspapers. After 10 minutes, the grout will be a little hard. Restir and smash the grout back to its original consistency.

5–9 Use a spatula to put some grout on the mosaic.

5–8 Mix grout to a thick smooth consistency. Note that the grout is much darker when wet. It will dry back to its original color.

5–10 Spread the grout firmly in a circular motion to fill all the gaps and push out the air bubbles.

NOTE: *If the grout is the wrong consistency, throw it away. You can't add water or powder once the grout has slaked. Retempering weakens the final product.*

7. Put on rubber gloves and place a dollop of grout on the mosaic (Photo 5–9) and, using the pads of your gloved fingers, mash the grout down into the joints in a circular motion (Photo 5–10). Press hard to force any air bubbles out by moving your hand in different directions to push the grout into all the little hidden spaces. Work quickly to avoid grout haze, but make sure it's done well.

8. Pay special attention to the edge of the mosaic. Make sure that the area where the tiles meet the base is sealed off by pushing grout into the spaces between the back of the tesserae and the base. Use the side of your fingers to bevel the grout between the two surfaces (Photo 5–11).

9. Use a spreader or the flat side of your finger to remove all the excess grout (Photo 5–12). This will

5–11 Use your fingers to smooth the edges, making sure to fill between the tile edges and the backing surface.

mean fewer rinses with the sponge. Check for air bubbles and fill any gaps that may appear. Lift the mosaic and fold back a layer of newspaper so you have a clean working space. You may want to do this several times during grouting.

10. Rinse your hands off in the bucket of water. Wet a sponge and then squeeze every drop of water out of it (Photo 5–13). Adding water on the grout will weaken it.

Tip: *Instead of using a sponge, you can also "dry clean" the mosaic by using pads of paper towel in a scuffing motion.*

5–12 Clean any excess grout off with a rubber-edged spreader.

5–13 Get rid of excess water from the sponge.

5–14 Pull the sponge firmly and flatly across the surface, using each side only once before rinsing again.

5–15 Be sure and clean the edges.

Tip: *I pat my wet gloved hands on newspaper after squeezing out the sponge. This keeps any excess water from running off the gloves onto the grout.*

CLEANING THE GROUT OFF AN UNEVEN SURFACE MOSAIC

It is a little more work to clean the grout off a mosaic with tesserae of varying heights. First, make sure all the spaces have been filled. Then clean the mosaic a few times with a full-size grout sponge. This will take most of the grout off, but it will also pull some of the grout from the higher tesserae areas to the lower tesserae areas. At this point, switch to a smaller sponge. If necessary, use a dental pick and even some cotton swabs to clean the lower tesserae.

5–16 Use paper towel for a final cleaning.

5–17 After the grout fully cures, apply a grout sealer.

11. Clean the grout off by pulling the damp sponge firmly and flatly across the surface (Photos 5–14 and 5–15). After a side has been used, turn the sponge over to a clean side or rinse it again. Wiping with a dirty sponge puts the grout back on and will make the cleaning job harder.

12. After the mosaic is fairly clean, use a pad of paper towel to lightly buff the surface of the mosaic and remove any smudges or smears (Photo 5–16).

13. Look closely at your mosaic. Use the dental tool to "excavate" the grout off any pieces that may be sitting lower or on an angle. Any remaining smudges can be removed with your finger. If any pieces need further polishing, do that now, too. If there are any air holes, fill them and clean again.

14. Set the mosaic aside to dry. Don't place it in front of a heater or in the sun. Cracking can occur if it cures too fast. If you're in a very hot or dry area, spray the mosaic lightly with a mister to slow down the drying. Repeat a few times a day. As the grout dries, the color will lighten back to the color of the powder. Allow the grout to cure for several days.

Sealing
15. Sponge on a penetrating grout sealer to protect the grout from stains and weather conditions (Photo 5–17). Several coats may be necessary. Repeat the sealing periodically to extend the life of the mosaic.

THE INDIRECT METHOD

The indirect, or reverse, method is a more complicated way of mosaicking. The mosaic is worked backwards like a mirror image. The tesserae are placed facedown using a temporary adhesive on a temporary mounting surface. To install, flip over the whole image (or sections of it) onto the permanent adhesive and base. The temporary mounting surface is then removed and the mosaic is seen facing the correct direction for the first time.

Although it is more work to create a mosaic by the indirect method, it's well worth it if conditions require. The main reasons for working in reverse are adverse working conditions, large projects, and the need for very flat surfaces. It's always more comfortable to create a mosaic in the studio rather than under awkward conditions onsite. For example, a fountain created using the direct method might require long sessions working on one's knees in order to apply the tesserae piece by piece. The indirect method makes it possible to install it all at one time. Large mosaics can be created in the studio in numbered sections and shipped on-site for installation. And because the mosaic is worked facedown, tesserae of different thickness can be used for a floor or tabletop. The adhesive is applied to the base at the correct depth for the thickest tesserae. When the mosaic is placed onto the adhesive, the thicker pieces stick deeper into the adhesive than the thinner ones, maintaining a flat surface. Working in reverse also offers an opportunity for making changes before the mosaic is final.

TEMPORARY MOUNTINGS AND ADHESIVES

There are several choices of temporary mountings and adhesives for use with the indirect method. The most common mounting is brown butcher or kraft paper. The design can be drawn directly on the paper—but backwards, remember. The tesserae are applied facedown with a water-soluble glue mixture. After the mosaic is flipped over and applied to the base, the paper is slowly soaked off and removed.

Several different temporary adhesives can be used to stick the tesserae to the paper. It's important that the adhesive be water soluble and easy to soak off. I use washable PVA, which is also called washable school glue. I buy the cheapest brand and add one-part water to three-parts glue. Control how much of this mix you use at a time, as it will cause the paper to buckle (see Tip). You can also use blue gel school glue without diluting. While this goes on very well, it is very gummy and messy when removing from the finished surface. Some mosaic artists use either a thin paste made from a mix of flour and water or thinned wallpaper paste. Both, however, can become brittle if the mosaic is moved a lot before installation.

Another option is LDPE (Low Density Polyethylene). LDPE is a clear and very sticky plastic sheeting that can be purchased from plastic manufacturers. It comes on huge rolls, so have the distributor cut it into a manageable size for you. Because LDPE is clear, you can lay it sticky-side up over the cartoon. The clear material allows you to lift up a corner and check your progress from the front.

Clear adhesive shelf paper is easier to get than LDPE, but it is not as sticky. The tesserae will tend to fall off during the mounting process.

Tip: *When working with kraft paper, tape the paper to the working surface with masking tape. Make sure the tape sticks all along every edge. Using a paintbrush, apply water lightly to the paper surface. The paper will shrink slightly while drying, which helps keep it from buckling while applying the tesserae. Don't worry if your paper does buckle; it will flatten back out after drying. Don't try substituting the kraft paper with brown grocery-bag paper. The grocery-bag paper is too thick and hard to soak off.*

ILLUSION TABLE
(INDIRECT METHOD)
LEVEL: INTERMEDIATE

MATERIALS
- Metal table stand with ¾-inch (19 mm) recess
- ⅝ inch (16 mm) wood base, cut to size
- Three shades of gray vitreous glass tile
- Three shades of white vitreous glass tile
- Natural gray sanded grout
- Washable school glue
- Tile mastic
- White vinegar and/or acid tile cleaner
- Penetrating grout sealer

TOOLS
- Brown kraft paper
- Wheeled cutters
- Small paintbrush
- Notched spreader
- Paper towels
- Small sponge
- Dental tool
- Grout sponge
- Rubber float
- Safety glasses
- Gloves

Prepare the Base and Design

1. Seal the wood on all six sides with a mixture of one-part PVA and four-parts water.

2. Cut the kraft paper slightly larger than the tabletop. Draw the design on the paper with a permanent marker. (Remember to draw it in reverse. You can hold your drawing up to a mirror to see how it'll look the other way.) Since this design is an optical illusion, it will be helpful to indicate where the colors go.

5–18 Cartoon, board, and tile colors.

Apply the Mosaic

3. Put on safety glasses. Use the wheeled cutters to cut in half some of the tiles from each shade of gray. Thin the washable glue with a little water. This makes paper removal easier. Use the paintbrush to apply the glue mixture to the front of the tile (Photo 5–19) or the kraft paper. One of the tricky things about working in the indirect method is that you're always looking at the back of the tile. Start on one side of the design and work to the other side, filling in each area with the appropriate color. Be sure to place the tiles smooth-side down, ridged-side up (Photo 5–20). Control the space between the tiles so that you leave room for grouting.

Background

4. After the central design is completed, cut into quarters some of the tiles from each shade of white. Leave some in half to use for the tapered pieces at the edge. Begin laying the pieces by outlining one side of the center shape. Randomly use the three shades of white. This will give depth to the background, which will enhance the optical illusion. Work the first side to the edges by repeating that line like a halo. Do the same on the second side (Photo 5–21).

Fix the Mosaic to the Base

5. After the mosaic has dried on the kraft paper, lift it up by two corners (Photo 5–22). Hold the paper tightly so it doesn't sag. Turn it over to check if a piece didn't get enough glue. It is better to have a piece fall off now than during the fixing process. Fix any loose pieces and allow to fully dry.

> **Tip:** *In cases where the mosaic is very large, either cut into sections or get a helper to flip the mosaic while the two of you hold it tightly to avoid sagging. If the placement of the mosaic is slightly off, use the rubber float to lightly smack the back of the paper in the direction it needs to shift.*

6. The first step of the mounting process is to pre-grout the piece from the back. Mix up the gray grout and, wearing gloves, gently apply to the back of the tiles (Photo 5–23). Fill all the joints and then, using a barely damp sponge, remove all the grout you can from the surface (Photo 5–24). This leaves the grout only in the joints. The grout will act as a barrier to the adhesive from reaching the actual top of the mosaic. Be especially careful about rubbing at the edges and loosening any tesserae. Cover the remaining grout that is in the container for possible touch-ups later.

7. Set the mosaic aside and quickly apply tile mastic to the board with a notched spreader (Photo 5–25). (I chose mastic because this is a small indoor table. If I was using the table for outdoors, or if it might be exposed to moisture, then I'd use cement-based adhesive.) Drag the spreader at a slight angle so that you scrape the teeth across the base, leaving grooves in the adhesive. The grooves allow the tesserae to settle evenly into the adhesive. Be sure to cover the board all the way to the edges.

8. Pick up the mosaic, turn it over, and align one corner to the corner of the board while holding most of the mosaic above the base. Once the corners are aligned, allow the mosaic to roll down onto the adhesive (Photo 5–26). As an alternative, turn the board over and press it onto the mosaic. Check the alignment on all sides and make any needed adjustments now. Notice that the paper is starting to look wet from the moisture in the grout.

9. Use the rubber float to lightly smack the mosaic into the adhesive (Photo 5–27). Work straight down and evenly across the surface, making sure that the tesserae are firmly and evenly embedded in the adhesive. Check the alignment once more, then use the sponge to moisten the paper backing (Photo 5–28). Be careful not to get the adhesive wet. Continue moistening the paper. As it gets damper, the imprint of the tesserae becomes clearer. After 15 minutes or so, gently lift a corner and check the adhesion. When the paper comes away easily, it's ready to remove (Photo 5–29). Have a dental tool handy to use on

5–19 Apply thinned washable glue to the tile front.

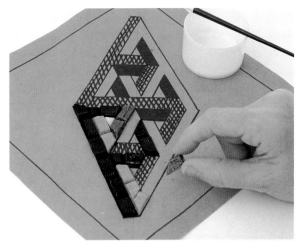

5–20 Place tile on the paper cartoon.

5–21 Paint a line of glue on the paper to lay the background.

5–22 After the tiles are applied and dried, lift the paper and check for loose tiles.

5–23 Pre-grouting from the back creates a barrier preventing the adhesive from reaching the top.

5–24 Gently clean off the back so that the tiles are exposed to ensure good adhesion.

5–25 Applying the mastic to the base.

5–26 Align the corners and roll the mosaic onto the adhesive.

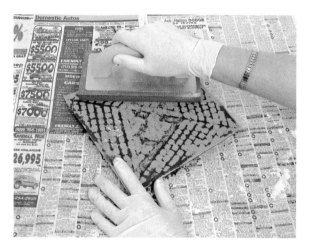

5–27 Lightly smack the mosaic with the rubber float to ensure a good bond.

5–28 Gently moisten the paper with a dampened sponge.

any stubborn glue. Note that this is a symmetrical design, so the orientation remains the same after installing in reverse.

10. Now that the paper is off you have two choices on regrouting. Regrouting is necessary because the pre-grouting will acquire small gaps as the mosaic is pressed into the adhesive and the paper is removed. The first and safest choice is to clean the surface gently with a barely damp sponge and let the adhesive dry overnight. Then you can safely regrout and clean. If you decide to do this, throw the reserved grout away and mix up a new batch the next day. The second choice is a little trickier and should only be done if you're very confident of the bond between the mosaic and the adhesive. While the adhesive is still wet, restir the reserved

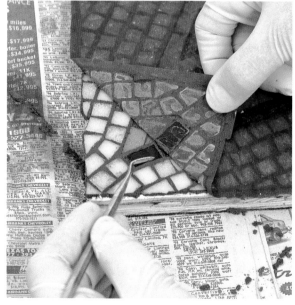

5–29 After the glue has loosened, peel the paper back flatly against the tile.

5–30 Regrout any gaps.

grout and gently rub over the surface to fill in any cracks in the grout (Photo 5–30). Clean with a barely damp sponge and leave to dry (Photo 5–31).

Finishing

11. After the mosaic is fairly clean, use a pad of paper towel to lightly buff the surface of the mosaic and remove any smudges or smears (Photo 5–32). After the grout and adhesive have fully cured, you may notice a slight grout haze across the surface of the tiles. Use a small sponge and white vinegar to wipe it off. If that doesn't work, use an acid tile cleaner. Follow the directions and be sure to wear protective gloves. Once the mosaic has fully cured, apply a penetrating grout sealer.

5–31 Gently but firmly pull the sponge flatly across the surface.

Assembling

12. Carefully place the mosaic into the top of the table frame (Photo 5–33). Pay special attention to the edges to avoid knocking any tiles out. The ⅝-inch (16-mm) board with vitreous tiles on top should be just even with the top of the ¾-inch (195-mm) recess.

5–32 When the mosaic is mostly clean, use a pad of paper towel to gently scuff over the surface for a final cleaning.

5–33 Lower the top gently onto the side supports.

DOUBLE-REVERSE METHOD

The double reverse method is useful when you might want to make a lot of changes as you create the mosaic. Draw your sketch normally, not in reverse. Then tape your sketch to the work surface and cover it with clear plastic shelf paper, sticky-side up. (Remove only a small portion of the protective paper at a time. The dust and residue from nipping the tiles can get on the shelf paper and quickly reduce its stickiness.) Place the back of the tesserae onto the sticky surface. As an alternative, press into a bed of Silly Putty to maintain maximum texture. After finishing the mosaic, apply LDPE, kraft paper, or cheesecloth with water-soluble glue to the top surface. Sandwich the mosaic between two boards and turn over. Remove the shelf paper and you now have a reverse mosaic that is ready for mounting.

5–34 Begin creating a double-reverse mosaic with texture by pressing the tesserae into Silly Putty.

MESH

Working on mesh is a variation of the direct method with many of the advantages of the indirect. You first glue the mosaic directly onto fiberglass mesh. Then you apply the adhesive to the base surface and press the mosaic on its mesh into it. This allows you to work direct in the studio and install elsewhere. It's especially good for large projects created off-site. And as long as tesserae of the same thickness are used, the surface will essentially be flat.

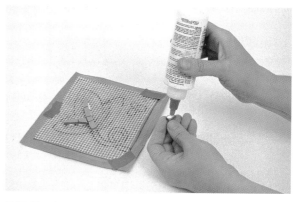

5–36 Glue the tesserae to the mesh using PVA glue.

SPLASH LEAF

1. Tape the sketch or cartoon onto the work surface with masking tape. Then tape a transparent plastic food-wrap over the drawing. (You can buy the plastic wrap at the grocery store.) The plastic wrap prevents the mesh from sticking to the drawing as you glue the tesserae. Finally, tape the mesh over the first two layers (Photo 5–35). You'll be able to see the drawing as you work.

2. Apply PVA (WeldBond) to each tessera and press it onto the mesh (Photo 5–36). Use enough glue to firmly anchor the piece to the mesh. Some of the mesh holes will remain open to allow a small amount of adhesive to go through and anchor the tesserae securely.

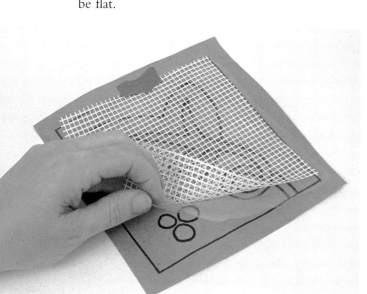

5–35 Tape the mesh over the plastic wrap which covers the design.

5–37 The mosaic on mesh before mounting.

Tip: *Mesh mosaic is a great way to dress up old ceramic bathroom or kitchen tile walls. Create some small mosaic insets the same size as the tiles. Remove some of the old tiles. Scrape the wall surface until it is thoroughly clean, apply the adhesive, and then install the mesh mosaic as a replacement. Grout using the same color as the rest of the wall.*

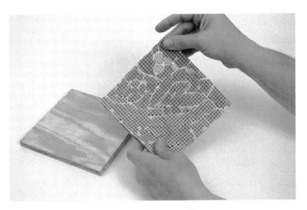

5–38 The mosaic from the back before mounting.

5–40 Align the corners and roll the mosaic down onto the adhesive.

5–39 Spread cement-based adhesive using a notched spreader.

5–41 Smack the mosaic with a rubber float to ensure a good bond.

3. Allow the glue to dry. Wait a few hours because the plastic wrap may prevent air from getting to the entire surface of the tile. Then turn the mosaic over and remove the plastic wrap so that the mosaic can finish drying (Photos 5–37 and 5–38).

4. Spread an adhesive, usually thinset mortar or mastic, over the base surface (Photo 5–39). Use a notched spreader to control the thickness. You want the adhesive to squish through the mesh but not seep high enough to interfere with the grouting.

5. Press the mosaic, mesh-side down, into the adhesive. Lightly smack the rubber float against the surface to ensure an even contact with the adhesive (Photos 5–40 and 5–41). Allow to dry.

6. Grout as usual. Seal if necessary.

EUROPE

CHAPTER

Europe has had a long tradition of mosaics since the ancient Greeks and Romans. These mosaics can be readily seen in museums, ruins, and places of worship. But Europe is not only home to a wealth of ancient mosaics, it is also the source for many contemporary trends. Mosaics are a frequent choice for public art and architectural features. One can visit a gallery and see a show of modern mosaics. Regular conferences and meetings of mosaicists are held in several European countries. New work and techniques are discussed, generating fresh ideas and collaborations.

In ancient times, Italy was home to the Romans who were the creators of a wealth of mosaics. Today, Italy is the center for new generations of mosaic artists who bring exciting and creative concepts to fine-art mosaics. Traditional marble and smalti are integrated with textural and sculptural elements. Schools in both Ravenna and Spilimbergo are training young mosaicists in both technique and aesthetics. Many of the finest mosaic materials are made in Italy and this ready supply of materials is used all over the world.

There are locales in Europe where artists created large-scale works of individual expression. In Spain, Gaudí and Jujol created the imaginative mosaics in Parc Güell. France is home to Maison Picassiette, which was created by Raymond Isidore. Perhaps the most exciting location is northwest of Rome in southern Tuscany. Niki de Saint Phalle built *Il Gardena dei Tarocchi* (*The Tarot Garden*), a park filled

Opposite Page: **Lucio Orsoni.** *Black and Grey Gold*, 1986. 43 x 43 inches (109 x 109 cm). Smalti, golds. Photo by the artist.

Above: **The Gallery at Orsoni.** Venice. Photo courtesy of Angelo Orsoni Srl.

with huge mosaic buildings and sculptures. The projects in this chapter draw on all these sources for inspiration. The degree of difficulty is graduated from easy to advanced. The different techniques are shown in depth.

Throughout this chapter are also many "Sites to See" lists that highlight Europe's long history of mosaic art. They are divided by area. Whether seeing ancient or contemporary mosaics is your goal, there are enough sites listed to keep you busy for many trips.

The gallery pages are rich with images from contemporary mosaicists working in a variety of mediums. Sculptural pieces, innovative public art projects, extensive pavements, and exciting textural works show how European artists are leading the way in exploring mosaics as a fine-art medium.

SITES TO SEE IN EUROPE

Austria	Vienna	Secessionist Building, Kunsthistorisches Museum, Hundertwasser House
Belgium	Brussels	Palais Stoclet
Croatia	Porec	Cathedral of Eufrasius
Cyprus	Paphos	House of Aion
Czech Republic	Prague	St. Vitus Cathedral
Denmark	Copenhagen	Kunstindustrimuseum
Germany	Berlin	Kaiser Wilhelm Gedachtnis Kirche, Berlin State Museum
	Darmstadt	Exhibition Hall
	Essen	Synagogue
	Frankfurt-am-Main	Dresdner Bank, Landeszentralbank
	Hamburg	Sankt Nikolai Church
	Trier	Reinsiches Landesmuseum
Netherlands	Ooosterhout	Theatre de Bussel
Portugal	Coimbra	Conimbrega
Sweden	Stockholm	City Hall
Switzerland	Fribough	Villa at Vallon

BLUE WILLOW TRAY

Level: Easy

Blue Willow china was imported to England during the mid–1800s and instantly became popular. Different versions of the pattern became a staple and many are all still readily available today. Blue Willow china is a favorite choice for mosaic artists working in the *picassiette* style. This tray uses elements of other blue and white china patterns to complement and emphasize the Blue Willow plate center.

Materials
- Wooden tray, painted white
- Variety of blue and white broken china
- Blue Willow plate center
- White sanded grout
- PVA glue (WeldBond)
- Penetrating grout sealer

Tools
- Small hammer
- Newspaper
- Side biter nippers
- Dental tool
- Masking tape
- Grout sponge
- Safety glasses
- Gloves
- Coarse sandpaper

Prepare the Base

1. If the painted finish of the tray is slick, scuff-sand it with coarse sandpaper.

Create the Tesserae

2. Put on safety glasses. Place plates or bowls face-down in a fold of newspaper. Use a small hammer and firmly tap the bottom rim through the paper (Photo 6–1). It will take some practice to learn the right amount of pressure. In addition, different types of china will require varying strengths. Lift the paper and check your progress. Once the pieces are broken into medium sizes, you may want to switch to nippers for more control (Photo 6–2). When you are done, pick up the folded paper by the corners for easy cleanup.

NOTE: *The center of the plate can be problematical because of the footplate. There are several choices in how to deal with it: you can nip the portion of the plate with the footplate off, you can use a grinder and grind it off, or you can buy a plate center already mounted on mesh from a mosaic supplier.*

Apply the China

3. Because this is a tray, try to use the flattest pieces possible. Cutting curved pieces smaller helps create a flatter surface. Glue the plate center to the middle of the tray. Surround it with a rim from another kind of plate (Photo 6–3). The corners are created from the rims and centers of saucers. The background is a different china in a squiggly blue-white pattern (Photo 6–4).

Grouting

4. Use masking tape to keep grout off the exposed tray sides. Grout as per instructions on pages 112–115. A white grout adds to the delicate feel of the blue and white china against the white tray.

Sealing

5. After the grout has cured, apply a penetrating grout sealer to prevent the grout from staining during use.

6–1 Break dishes by placing each facedown in a fold of newspaper, then crack on the rim with a hammer.

6–2 Use side biters to nip plate rim.

6–3 Place rim around plate center.

6–4 After creating the corners, fill in the background.

SITES TO SEE IN ITALY

Aquileia	Basilica, Archeological Museum, Paleo-Christian Museum
Cefalu	Cathedral
Cervia	Floating Carpet Fountain
Florence	Medici Chapel, Museum Museo Pietra Dura, Cathedral, San Miniato al Monte, Baptistry of San Giovanni, Uffizi Gallery
Herculaneum	Archeological site
Milan	Chapel of Sant Aquilino, San Lorenzo Maggiore, Basilica di San Ambrogio
Monreale	Cathedral
Murano	Basilica dei Santi Maria e Donato
Naples	Museo Nazionale, San Gennaro Cathedral
Orvieto	Cathedral
Ostia	Ostia Antica
Otranto	Cathedral
Palermo	Palantine Chapel, Royal Palace, La Martorana
Palestrina	Museo Nazionale Archeologico Prenestino
Piazza Amerina	Roman Villa Casale
Pisa	Cathedral
Pompeii	Archeological site
Ravenna	Parco della Pace, Mausoleo di Galla Placidia, National Museum, Saint Appolinare in Classe, Saint Appolinare Nuovo, San Giovanni, San Vitale, Arian Baptistry, Neonian Baptistry, Archepiscopalian Chapel
Rome	St Paul's Within the Walls, San Clemente, Santa Maria in Cosmedin, Sant'Agostino, Santa Pudenziana, St. Peters, S Giovanni Laterano, Santa Maria in Dominica, Santi Cosma e Damiano, St. Lorenzo-fuori-la-mura, Santa Cecilia in Travestere, Santa Maria in Travestere, Sant'Agnese fuori le Mura, Santa Maria Maggiore, Santa Costanza, Vatican Museum, National Roman Museum, Basilica of St. Praxedes
Russi	Archeological site
Spoleto	Cathedral
Tarquinia (near)	Il Gardena dei Tarocchi
Tivoli	Hadrian's Villa
Torcello	Santa Maria Assunta Basilica
Venice	San Marco, Casino, Lido, Palazzo Barbarigo, Salviati Headquarters

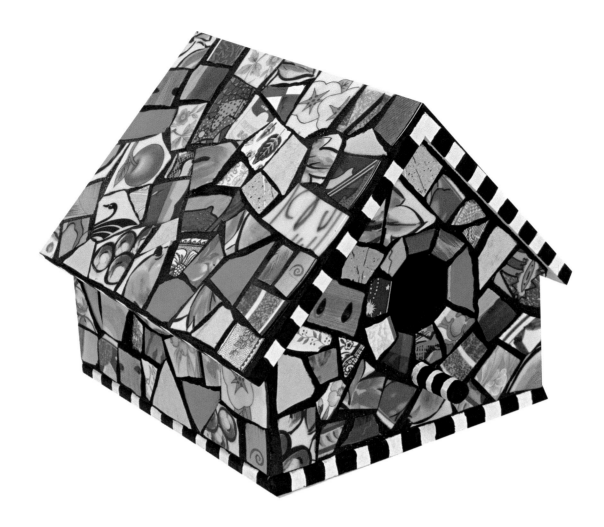

MAISON POUR OISEAUX

LEVEL: INTERMEDIATE

This birdhouse draws on inspiration from Maison Picassiette in Chartres, France. Raymond Isidore, a grave sweeper, picked up some pieces of broken china and glass on a walk in the late 1930s. That was the start of a project that continued till 1962. He mosaicked the inside and outside of his house, the courtyards, the garden, the walkways, and even the coffee grinder. It is a place of great joy. This birdhouse uses brightly colored bits of china to bring a little of Maison Picassiette home.

MATERIALS
• Plain wooden birdhouse
• Variety of brightly colored broken china
• Black sanded grout
• Black and white acrylic paint
• Tile mastic adhesive
• PVA glue (WeldBond)

TOOLS
• Side biter nippers
• Hammer
• Newspaper
• Craft sticks
• 2-inch (5-cm) sponge brush
• Narrow, flat paintbrush
• Dental tool
• Masking tape
• Grout sponge
• Safety glasses

 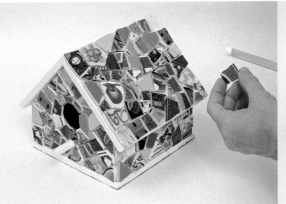 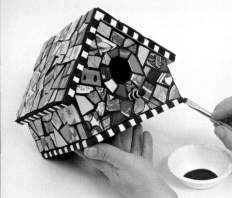

6–5 Seal the birdhouse with the mix of PVA and water. *6–6* Apply the china pieces with mastic. *6–7* Paint black stripes on the trim.

Prepare the Base

1. Seal all the exposed surfaces of the birdhouse with a sponge brush and mixture of one-part PVA glue and four-parts water (Photo 6–5). After it has dried, paint the edges white.

Apply the China

2. Put on safety glasses. Nip the china into random pieces of a similar size. As an alternative, you can place the china in a fold of the newspaper and crack lightly with a hammer.

3. Using a craft stick, apply the mastic to the back of each piece and place it on the birdhouse in a random fashion (Photo 6–6). Mix colors evenly across each surface and try to keep the grout lines reasonably consistent. The mastic will keep the tesserae from sliding and allow you to build up the back if a piece is extremely uneven. Since this a decorative piece, water resistance isn't an issue. Use the dental pick to clean off any mastic that may have squished out from the side of a piece. This allows you to set the tessera next to it closely.

Grouting

4. Use masking tape to keep the grout off the remaining exposed wood. Grout as per instructions on pages 112–115. Because the colors of the china are strong, I chose a black-colored grout to further enhance them. Before the grout dries, remove the masking tape by peeling it away from the grout and smooth over any rough places with your finger.

Painting the Trim

5. After the grout has fully cured, use the white paint to touch up any dark spots on the trim. Then use the black paint to create stripes on the trim and perch (Photo 6–7).

SITES TO SEE IN FRANCE

Chartres	Maison Picassiette
Ganagobie	Monastery
Nice	Faculty of Law, Chagall Museum
Paris	Louvre, Pasteur Institute, Sacré-Coeur, National Opera, UNESCO House, Tomb of Rudolf Nureyev at St. Geneviève des Bois Russian Cemetery
Pau (near)	Seviac
Rouen	Museum of Antiquities
Vienne	Museum Lapidaire, Saint-Romain-en-Gal

GÜELL TURTLE
LEVEL: INTERMEDIATE

Antoni Gaudí created many unique three-dimensional mosaic animals in Parc Güell, Barcelona. One of them was a large lizard in which water flows from its mouth (see page 53). Our turtle has a lot of humor too, especially in its tail. Using abalone for its shell is a natural way to add a tactile aspect to the piece. Using garden statuary as the base makes it easy for anyone to create mosaic sculpture. Because this project is three-dimensional, it will be trickier to mosaic.

MATERIALS
• Cement statuary turtle (found in garden centers)
• Tumbled abalone shell pieces
• Vitreous glass tiles in lime green
• Iridescent glass tiles in purple
• Black unglazed ceramic tile
• Thinset cement mortar with admix
• Dark gray sanded grout
• Penetrating grout sealer

TOOLS
• Wheeled cutters
• Palette knife
• Dental tool
• Grout sponge
• Safety glasses
• Gloves
• Masking tape
• Coarse sandpaper
• Dust mask

Tip: *Don't cut all your tiles up into small pieces. Always save some whole ones so that you can cut that odd shape that you may occasionally need.*

Prepare the Base

1. Wearing protective gloves, apply a coating of thinset cement to smooth out any bumps on the turtle. Allow the cement to cure overnight. If necessary, use coarse sandpaper to smooth any rough places. Be sure to wear a dust mask when you do this.

Apply the Shell

2. Use thinset cement and a palette knife to butter the back of each abalone shell before you apply it (Photo 6–8). Continue working from the top down to the edge, fitting the odd-shaped pieces of shell together. Use enough thinset to self-grout the shell.

Cover the Underbelly

3. Use the wheeled cutters to shape the purple tiles into rectangles and triangles. Use them to cover the bottom half of the turtle. Cut some of the lime tiles to create the tail before finishing the back end (Photo 6–9).

Head and Legs

4. Cut two small circles from the black tile for the eyes and apply. Create an inventory of random shapes from the lime green tiles and cover one leg at a time and finally the head. Fitting different angles together will help taper the nose.

Grouting

5. Use masking tape to cover the back of the turtle. Grout as per instructions on pages 112–115. I chose a dark gray grout to pull the turtle base together with the thinset used to apply the shells. I did not grout the back, as it would be difficult to clean the abalone shell. Before the grout dries, carefully remove the masking tape by pulling back flatly and away from the grout. This will allow you to repair any unevenness on the edges of the grout before it dries.

Sealing

6. After the grout has fully cured, seal with a penetrating grout sealer.

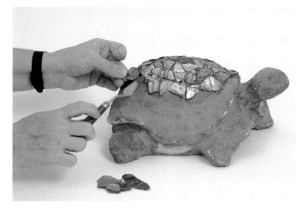

6–8 Use palette knife to apply thinset to abalone pieces for the turtle's shell.

6–9 Work the tail in the lime green.

SITES TO SEE IN THE UNITED KINGDOM

Bath	Roman baths
Chichester	Bignor Regis, Fishbourne
Cirencester	Corinium
Exeter	Public Art, Exeter Museum
Leeds	City Museum, Church of St. Aidan
London	British Museum, National Gallery, Leicester House, Tottenham Court Underground Station, The Gilbert Collection at Somerset House, St. Paul's Cathedral, Westminster Cathedral

ADAM AND EVE

LEVEL: ADVANCED

The Romans created myriad emblemata featuring the human form. This mosaic of Adam and Eve draws its inspiration from these figures while adding a little humor to the traditional subject. Notice that Eve's eyes are caught glancing up at the snake.

MATERIALS
- 16-inch (41-cm) round wooden base
- Vitreous glass tiles in a variety of colors (brown, beige, tan, flesh tones, different greens, blues, and lavenders)
- Tan sanded grout
- PVA glue (like WeldBond)

TOOLS
- Side biter nippers
- Wheeled cutters
- 2-inch (5-cm) sponge brush
- Carbon paper
- Sketch paper
- Pencil and permanent marker
- Dental tool and tweezers
- Safety glasses
- Grout sponge and gloves

Tip: *When working with small bits of vitreous glass tile, you'll often find that the beveled edge may cause a the tessera to tip over. I use a small shard of tile as a shim to support the tile as the glue dries. As long as the shim doesn't stick out too far, it can just remain under the piece permanently.*

6–10 Darken the design with a permanent marker and then begin selecting tan colors for skin tones.

6–11 Use tweezers to apply the small pieces.

Prepare the Base

1. Seal all exposed surfaces with a sponge brush and a mixture of one-part PVA glue and four-parts water.

2. Draw your design on a sketch paper and then use carbon paper to transfer it to the base. Your design doesn't have to be an exact duplicate of the one shown. Use a permanent marker to darken the lines, except if the tesserae are translucent (Photo 6–10). When working with faces or other detailed motifs, it's very helpful to use as large a base as possible. The smaller the base, the smaller and more challenging the features.

The Faces

3. Put on your safety glasses. Use the wheeled cutters and side biters to cut odd shapes from the brown, beige, and tan tiles. Begin working on Eve's head from the top down (Photo 6–11). Follow the design's guidelines. Apply glue to the base and position each tile. Use the dental pick to clean off any excess glue that may squish out. This allows you to set the next piece closer.

Finish Laying Tesserae

4. Continue working on Eve by applying darker tones into areas with shadows and paler tones where the light would hit. After finishing Eve, do the same on Adam except use slightly larger and squarer pieces to give a masculine feel to his form. After the key fig-

ures are done, work the tree limb, snake, and apple. Continue to the vines and leaves and finally the background.

Grouting

5. Grout as per instructions on pages 112–115. On this project, I chose a tan-colored grout to pull the skin tones together. While that works, notice how the light grout tends to fracture the background. An alternative would be to grout the bodies first and rub a darker color into the background. This can be tricky and takes some practice.

SITES TO SEE IN SPAIN

Ampurias	Archeological site
Barcelona	Palau de la Musica Catalonia, Casa Battló, Church of Sagrada Familia, Parc Güell, La Pedrera, Museo d'Arqueologia, Liceu Metro Station
Cordova	Cathedral, Great Mosque, Mihrab
Merida	Cosmological mosaic
Seville	Italica
Tarragona	Mausoleum of Centcelles

GRAPEVINE BACKSPLASH

LEVEL: ADVANCED

The Art Nouveau movement emphasized flowing lines and motifs from nature. Grapevines were a popular subject for artists. This backsplash is an updated interpretation featuring stylized vines, leaves, and bunches of grapes. The mesh technique is more advanced but very doable when broken down into manageable steps.

MATERIALS
- 2-inch (5-cm) matte ceramic tiles in mustard yellow
- 2-inch (5-cm) glossy ceramic tiles in two colors of maroon
- 2-inch (5-cm) glossy ceramic tiles in two colors of dark green
- 2-inch (5-cm) glossy ceramic tiles in light green
- Fiberglass mesh
- Dark tan sanded grout
- PVA glue (WeldBond)
- Tile mastic
- Penetrating grout sealer

TOOLS
- Brown kraft paper
- Clear plastic food wrap
- Masking tape
- Pro scorer/breaker
- Side biter nippers
- Utility knife
- Grooved spreader
- Rubber float
- Pencil and permanent marker
- Rubber spreader
- Grout sponge
- Dental tool
- Masking tape
- Safety glasses
- Gloves

Tip: *Always work the focal areas first. Then work out from those or from top to bottom or side to side. This helps you to avoid working into a corner, which often tempts you to use some odd-shaped pieces to finish.*

Create the Cartoon

1. Use a large piece of brown kraft paper to create an exact template of the wall area to be covered. Be sure to note where outlets or switches are. Draw the design directly onto the paper template and use a permanent marker to darken the lines.

2. Tape down the cartoon to the work surface. Tape the clear plastic food wrap over the template and then the mesh on top. You should be able to easily see the design through the plastic.

The Vines

3. Use the scorer/breaker to cut some of the green and maroon tiles in half. Then use side biters to cut the shapes you need: round grapes of varying sizes, narrow green pieces for vines and curlicues, and tapered light-greens for the veins of the leaves. Glue the tesserae to the mesh using PVA glue. Use enough glue to firmly anchor the piece but be sure to keep the joints clear for grouting.

Background

4. After the central design is completed, use the scorer/breaker to cut the mustard tiles into angular halves. Use the nippers to create triangles, parallelograms, and other odd shapes. Start working the background from one side to the other (Photo 6–12). Try and keep a consistent rhythm between the size of the pieces as well as the grout lines. Be careful to avoid creating long breaks or grout rivers

that will distract from your design. As you come to any switches or outlets, leave enough of an edge for the cover to go over it easily. Leave ¼ inch (6 mm) at the edge all the way around for grouting. Let dry overnight.

Tip: *Once the sections are cut, lift and turn them over. This will allow you to check whether any pieces aren't glued on well. You will also be able to remove the plastic wrap and allow air to get to all the glue so it completely dries.*

Create Sections

5. You have two choices for cutting the mosaic into sections for mounting. If your worktable isn't big enough for the whole design, finish a section plus a little more, and then use a utility knife or other sharp blade to cut between the tiles to create sections. It is important to cut even sections as it will make the mounting easier. It would be ideal if your worktable was large enough to hold the whole design. Then you could easily judge where the cuts should go. Regardless, sections should be no larger than you can easily handle by yourself. I usually cut no larger than approximately an 18-inch (46-cm) square.

Installation

6. Make sure that the wall is smooth and free of

6–12 After creating the vines and grapes, start filling in the background.

6–13 Apply mastic with notched spreader. Note spacers at the bottom.

texture or dirt. Start the installation at the bottom and work up the surface. This prevents the sections from sliding down the wall. If the backsplash has under-cabinet areas on either side, install these areas first and then work across the bottom. Pay special attention to the spacing. If the template was made accurately, it should fit together perfectly.

> **Tip:** *I use a few scrap tiles under the bottom edge to maintain a consistent space for grouting later on.*

7. Working a section at a time, use a notched spreader to apply mastic over the area to be covered (Photo 6–13). Press firmly with the spreader in order to limit the depth of the adhesive.

This prevents the mastic from filling the joints where the grout will be. I chose to use mastic on this project, but thinset cement would work just as well.

8. Hold the section by the two top corners. Line one corner up while holding the other side away from the adhesive (Photo 6–14). Slowly roll the section onto the wall and line up the other side (Photo 6–15). If the section is slightly off, use the rubber float to gently push it into place. When the position is right, gently smack the entire section flatly with the float to firmly fix it in the adhesive (Photo 6–16). Continue fitting the mosaic together section by section (Photo 6–17). Check the depth of the adhesive and use a dental tool to clean out any excess before it hardens. Allow 24 hours to dry before grouting.

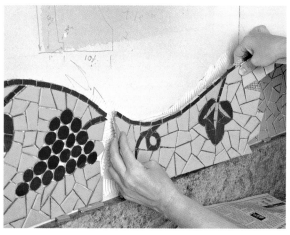

6–14 Align the section on the wall.

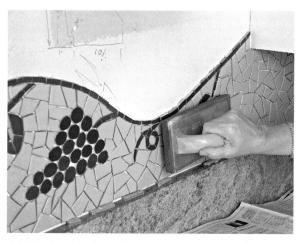

6–16 Use the rubber float to firmly seat the section in the adhesive.

6–15 Roll the section onto the adhesive.

6–17 Roll the section onto the adhesive.

Grouting

9. Pull out the pieces of scrap tile used to establish spacing along the bottom edge. Use masking tape to protect the cabinets from the grout. Cover the stove area with newspaper and use masking tape to hold it to the bottom edge.

10. Grout as per instructions on pages 112–115. On this project, I chose a dark tan grout (Photo 6–18). It unites the background without fracturing the look of the vines and grapes. Use the squeegee to remove any excess grout (Photo 6–19). This means fewer rinses of the sponge. Then clean the grout off with a damp sponge (Photo 6–20). Use one side of the sponge to clean and then turn it over to the other clean side and then rinse again. Wiping with a dirty sponge will put the grout back on and make the cleaning job harder. Be sure to squeeze every drop of water from the sponge and press hard.

11. Use a pad of paper towels to lightly buff the surface of the mosaic, removing any remaining smudges (Photo 6–21).

12. After the mosaic has been cleaned, remove the masking tape by peeling it down and away from the grout (Photo 6–22). This prevents the tape from pulling out any chunks of grout. While the grout is still wet, use your finger to smooth any rough spots the tape left.

Sealing

13. Allow the grout to cure for several days and then sponge on a penetrating grout sealer to protect the grout from stains (Photo 6–23). Several coats may be necessary.

6–18 Firmly spread grout into the joints using a circular motion. Note that the grout is darker when wet.

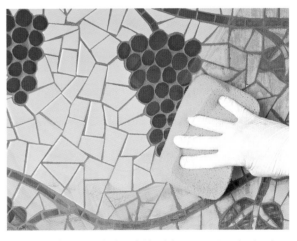

6–20 Clean firmly with the broad side of the sponge. Press hard and use a clean side for each swipe.

6–19 Scrape all the excess grout off the surface.

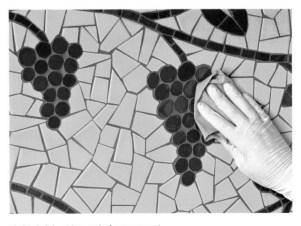

6–21 Polish with a pad of paper towel.

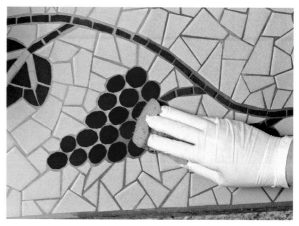

6–22 Remove masking tape by pulling down and away from the mosaic.

6–23 After curing, use a small sponge to apply sealer to the grout.

6–24 Detail showing an electrical outlet.

Sites to See in Greece

Ancient Corinth	Archeological site and museum
Athens	Church of Saint Erini, Monastery of Daphni
Chios	Monastery of Nea Moni
Crete	Kasyelli Kisamon
Daphni	The Catholicon
Delos	House of Dionysus
Eretria	House of Mosaics
Island of Delos	Archeological site
Pella	Archeological site and museum
Olynthos	Archeological site
Salonika	Church of Hosios David, St. Demetrius, Hagios Georgios, Santa Sofia
Thebes	Monastery of St. Luke of Stiris

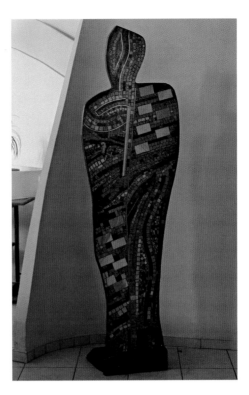

Above Left: **Alexandr Kornookhov.** Stone, gold, smalti. Parco del Pace, Ravenna, Italy. Photo by author.

Above Right: **George Trak.** *Figure*, 1992. 7 feet (2 m). Mosaic and stainless steel. Photo by the artist.

Right: **Sally Imbert.** *Gateway of the Sun* (detail). Unglazed ceramic, vitreous glass, mirror, stained glass. Photo by the artist.

Above: **Cleo Mussi.** *Twin Cats*, 1999. 3 x 1 feet (100 x 30 cm). Recycled china. Photo by the artist.

Right: **Norma Vondee.** *Sister 1*, 2000. 6 feet x 2 feet x 1.5 inches (1.8 m x 0.6 m x 3.8 cm). Ceramic, vitreous glass. Photo by the artist.

Opposite Page: **Rossella Baccolini.** *Selene*, 1991. 5.6 x 5.6 feet (1.7 x 1.7 m). Smalti, marble, clay, cotton. Photo by the artist.

Right: **Rosalind Wates.** *Mosaic Mackerel*, 1996. 16.4 feet (5 m). Pebbles, glass, mussel shells. Photo by the artist.

Below **Martin Cheek.** *Leaping Frog*, 1999. 35 x 57 inches (90 x 144 cm). Smalti, vitreous, mirror, beach glass, stained glass, pebbles. Photo by the artist.

Opposite Page: **Dugald MacInnes.** *Megalithic Alignment* (Venus in Conjunction: Harvest), 2001. Scottish/Welsh slate, golds. Photo by the artist.

Above: **Iliev Iliya Ivanov.** *Balkan Melody*, 2001. 47 x 47 feet (120 x 120 cm). Stone and oxide color. Photo by the artist.

Opposite Page, Top Left: **Iliev Iliya Ivanov.** *The Black Beach*, 1991. 3.3 x 2.6 feet (1 m x .80 cm). Stone and sea stone. Photo by the artist.

Opposite Page, Bottom Left: **Iliev Iliya Ivanov.** *Winter at Carbondale*, 1991. 40 x 32 inches (100 x 80 cm). Silicate forms and stone. Photo by the artist.

Opposite Page, Far Right: **Elaine M. Goodwin.** *He*, 1999. 6.2 x 2.5 x 0.3 feet (1.9 m x .80 cm x 10 cm). Carrara marble, antique gold, smalti, fool's gold. Photo by John Melville.

Top Left: **Eric Rieusset Cros.** *Lou Aguieloun (Provencal Wind)*, 2001. Tile, mirror. Photo by the artist.

Below Left: **Tessa Hunkin.** *Romford Market Mosaic* (detail), 1999. 3.3 x 656 feet (1 x 200 m). Ceramic. Photo by the artist.

Below Right: **Marcelo de Melo.** *American Beauty*, 2000. 32 x 14 inches (80 x 35 cm). Ceramic, china, pebbles. Photo by Paola Lazcano.

Opposite Page, Top: **Sally Imbert, Claire Cotterill, and the residents at Willow House.** *Sunflower Garden Furniture.* 4 x 7 feet (1.25 x 2 m). Ceramic and glass. Photo by the artist.

Opposite Page, Bottom: **Noelle M. Horsfield.** *Abundant Tree Table*, 2001. 48 x 31 x 22.5 inches (122 x 79 x 57 cm). Vitreous glass. Photo by the artist.

Top: **Robert Field.** *Fusion of Green*, 2001. 24 x 18 inches (61 x 46 cm). Glazed and unglazed ceramic, vitreous glass. Photo by the artist.

Center: **Chrissie Woods.** *Al Fresco*, 2000. 22 x 17 inches (55 x 43 cm). Unglazed ceramic, vitreous glass, smalti, marble, glass fusions, beach pebbles. Photo by the artist.

Bottom: **Zantium Mosaics.** *Brook Trout*. 43 x 22 inches (110 x 55 cm). Vitreous glass. Photo by Michael Taylor.

Opposite Page: **Jo Letchford.** *Neptune*, 2001. 32 x 14 x 11 inches (81 x 35 x 28 cm). Ceramic, vitreous glass, glass nuggets, beads, aquarium gravel, shells. Photo by Colin Bowling.

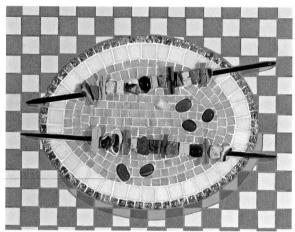

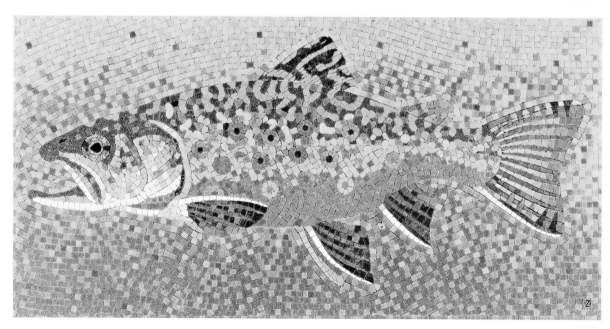

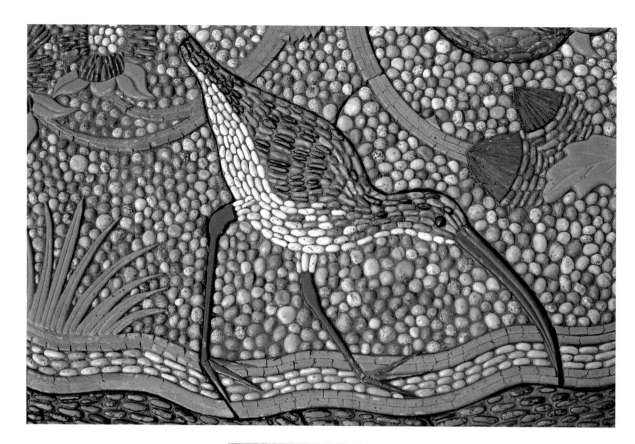

Above: **Maggy Howarth.** *Paradise Garden*
(detail), 1998. 26-foot (8-m) diameter. Pebbles.
Photo by Jim Rubery.

Right: **Maggy Howarth.** *Butterfly*, 1996.
4-foot (1.2-m) diameter. Pebbles. Photo by
the artist.

Opposite Page: **Manfred Hoehn.** *Sonnen-
blume (Sunflower)*, 1969. 2.3 x 2 feet (70 x
60 cm). Venetian flat mosaic, glass cakes, marble. Photo by the artist.

Top Right: **Chrissie Woods.** *Stargate*, 2001. Glass, golds, pyrite, hematite, slate. Photo by the artist.

Bottom Right: **Oliver Budd.** *Cats and Bug in Key-Cut Rug*, 2001. 1.2 square yards (1 sq. m). Ceramic. Photo by the artist.

Top Left: **Liz d'Ath.** Susi Earnshaw Theatre School, London. Photo by the artist.

Bottom Left: **Doreen Mastrandrea.** *Entryway* (detail), 1999. 3 x 4 feet (91 x 122 cm). Ceramic, pottery. Photo by the artist.

Opposite Page: **Cleo Mussi.** *Green Fingered Lady*, 1998. 3 x 1.5 x 1.3 feet (82 x 46 x 40 cm). Recycled china. Photo by Jens Storch.

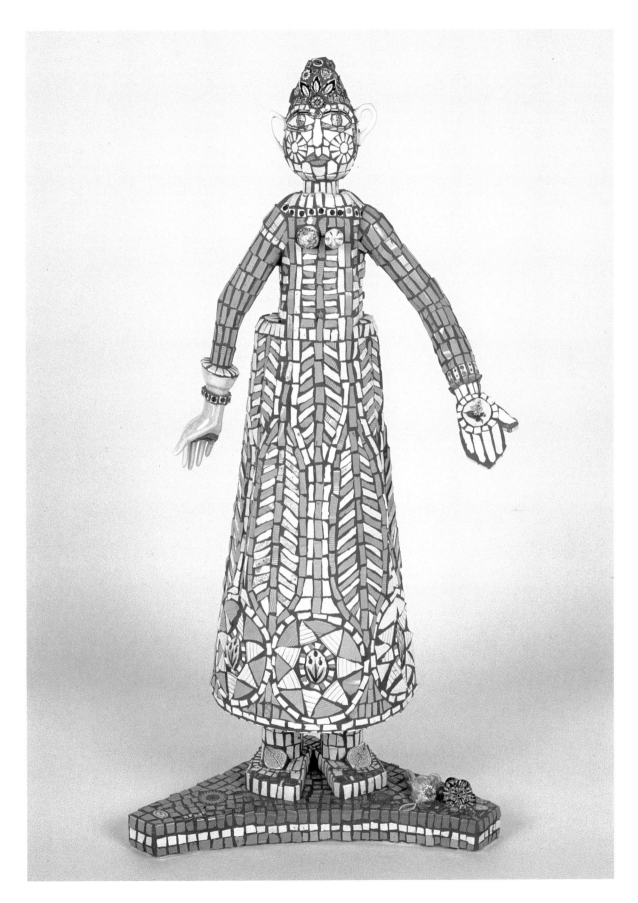

Ken Knowlton. *American Gothic*, 1991. 32 x 26 inches (81 x 66 cm) each. Seashells. Photo by the artist.

THE AMERICAS

Above: **Sonia King.** *Prickle Down Theory*, 2001. 17 x 10 x 7 inches (43 x 25 x 18 cm). Glass, ceramic, pebbles. Photo by author.

While Europe certainly has claim to the longest tradition of mosaic art, artists in the Americas have unbounded freedom of expression. The melting pots of the United States and Canada draw on traditions from around the world yet interpret them with fresh eyes.

Mosaicists in the Western Hemisphere constantly push the envelope, showing a willingness to use unusual materials in new ways. Broken safety glass, the letter keys from computer keyboards, and discarded watch faces are just a few of the unique tesserae cleverly used in "trash to treasure" mosaics. For example, Isaiah Zagar uses recycled tile and found objects to enliven South Street in Philadelphia.

Pre-Columbian cultures created mosaics from tiny tesserae of turquoise and other semi-precious stones. Today, in Brazil, artists continue to create mosaics from gemstones and minerals. Many of Mexico's great muralists, like Diego Rivera, designed huge mosaics as architectural accents for public buildings. These large-scale mosaics express cultural and political points of view.

The projects in this section were inspired from motifs firmly rooted in the Americas region. The gallery pages are full of innovative work in a variety of materials. Shown are the popularity of handmade tesserae and stained glass that are used in different ways. Mosaics on ceilings, floors, furniture and objects offer lots of ideas. The "Sites to See" lists highlight these many places, including inventive public art murals and sculptures that are worth seeing.

PENNY POT
LEVEL: EASY

This project can be made very quickly, as coins offer different colors and sizes of tesserae without cutting. Play around with different currencies and patterns to create your own pots.

MATERIALS
- Heavy clay pot
- Coins in two colors (pennies and nickels)
- Thinset cement mortar with admix
- Black sanded grout
- Penetrating grout sealer

TOOLS
- Palette knife
- Dental tool
- Grout sponge
- Gloves

Apply the Coins
1. Use the palette knife to apply thinset to a small area at a time. This prevents the thinset from getting too dry for a proper bond. Be sure to control the depth of the mortar to avoid having it squish up between the coins. It may take some practice to get the right depth. Press each coin firmly into the thinset, and then give it a little twist as you seat it (Photo 7–1). This ensures a tight bond. Work one row at a time. As the pot widens and then narrows again, you may have to adjust the spacing. Use the dental pick to clean off any excess cement that may have pressed out.

Grouting
2. While grouting isn't absolutely necessary on this piece (Photo 7–2), the black really sets off the coins and enhances the pattern. After the mortar has fully cured, be sure to seal the pot inside and out with a penetrating grout sealer.

7–1 Apply thinset to coins and press onto pot.

7–2 Ungrouted penny pot.

SITES TO SEE IN THE UNITED STATES

Baltimore, MD	Baltimore Museum of Art, Taylor Manor Hospital
Boston, MA	Park St. Subway Station
Chicago, IL	Chagall Mosaic, First National
Coney Island, NY	O'Grady School
Dallas, TX	Dallas Museum of Art, St. Jude Chapel, Hall of State at Fair Park, Children's Medical Center
Denver, CO	Denver International Airport
Fort Worth, TX	Kimbell Art Museum
Lincoln, NE	State Capitol
Los Angeles, CA	Watts Towers, Home Savings of America at Figueroa and 7th
Mitchell, SD	Corn Palace
New York, NY	Metropolitan Museum of Art, Chambers Street Subway Station, 59th St./Lexington Ave. Subway Station, Spring Street Subway Station, Times Square/42nd Street Subway Station, Hudson Street Subway Station
Orlando, FL	Charles Hosmer Morse Museum of American Art, Magic Kingdom in Disney World, Orlando Airport
Oxford, MS	Mary Buie Museum
Palo Alto, CA	Stanford Memorial Church
Philadelphia, PA	South Street, Physicians for Social Responsibility Bldg., Curtis Publishing, United States Mint (lobby)
Phoenix, AZ	Heard Museum
Princeton, NJ	Princeton University Art Museum
San Diego, CA	Horton Plaza
Spokane, WA	Worlds Fair Expo
St. Louis, MO	Cathedral Basilica
Tampa, FL	Administrative Building at the University S. Florida
Washington, DC	Dumbarton Oaks Museum
Worcester, MA	Worcester Art Museum

FLUTTERBY GARDEN STAKE

LEVEL: EASY

Mirror is a readily available material that really sparkles outside in the garden. Mix it with iridescent stained glass and marble gems for an eye-catching addition to your yard. A variety of metal forms on stakes are now available from garden centers. The stakes are usually made in two pieces. Just mosaic the top and reinsert the stake on the back.

MATERIALS
• Butterfly garden stake (found in garden centers)
• Blue, green, and silver iridescent flat-back marbles
• Blue and turquoise iridescent stained glass
• Mirror tiles
• Black sanded grout
• Two-part quick-setting epoxy
• Rust-preventing black paint

• Penetrating grout sealer

TOOLS
• Glass scorer
• Running pliers
• Wheeled cutters
• Craft sticks
• Tweezers
• Safety glasses
• Grout sponge
• Gloves

Prepare the Base
1. If the base and stake are rusty, remove all the rust. Then spray the top and bottom of the butterfly, plus the stake, with a rust-preventing black paint.

2. Put on safety glasses. Use the glass scorer and running pliers to create small mirror tesserae. Just carefully score and snap the needed sizes and shapes. Using wheeled cutters to trim the shapes.

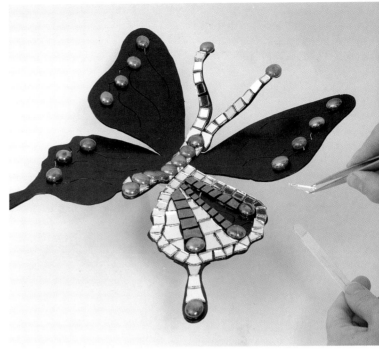

7–3 Apply the marble gems and mirror to the body and antennae.

7–4 Use tweezers to apply narrow mirror tesserae.

Apply the Mosaic

3. Apply the silver marbles to the body and ends of the antennae with a quick-setting epoxy (Photo 7–3). Use small triangles of mirror to fill around the marbles and small squares down the antennae. When working with quick-setting epoxy, there isn't much time to change your mind, so be ready to place the tesserae once the epoxy is mixed and applied with a craft stick. Mix a small batch at a time, as the epoxy quickly becomes unusable. Some epoxies have a very strong odor, so always work in a well-ventilated area. You may want to consider using a respirator. If you're prone to getting adhesive on your skin, wear latex gloves while working.

4. Add the green and turquoise marbles to the wings and use small square mirrors to outline the wings (Photos 7–4 and 7–5). Use turquoise stained glass to make lines from the body to the marbles on the bottom wings. Repeat for the top wings using the blue glass. Fill in the empty spaces by fitting tapered mirror pieces between the rows (Photos 7–4 and 7–5). Tweezers are very handy for this.

7–5 Outline wings with mirror squares.

Grout

5. Follow the grouting instructions on pages 112–115. I chose a black grout to create the illusion that the "flutterby" is flying. Only the sparkly bits show up outdoors.

Sealing

6. After the grout has fully cured, apply a penetrating grout sealer before placing outside.

SUN GOD

LEVEL: INTERMEDIATE

The sun is a symbol that is used repeatedly in Latin and South America. It is also a popular subject for mosaicists. Choose from a variety of materials to create your own sun god for the garden.

MATERIALS

- Terra-cotta or cement sun (found in garden centers)
- 2-inch (5-cm) matte ceramic tiles, frost-proof, yellow-gold
- 1-inch (2.5-cm) glossy ceramic tiles, frost-proof, burnt orange
- 1-inch (2.5-cm) glossy ceramic tiles, frost-proof, red-orange
- 1-inch (2.5-cm) glossy ceramic tiles, frost-proof, blue
- 1-inch (2.5-cm) glossy ceramic tiles, frost-proof, white

- Thinset cement mortar with admix
- Terra-cotta-color sanded grout
- Penetrating grout sealer

TOOLS

- Side biter nippers
- Pro scorer/breaker
- Palette knife
- Pencil
- Dental tool
- Grout sponge
- Gloves
- Safety glasses

7–6 Apply features to thinset-smoothed base.

7–7 Complete one side of the face and then match the other side.

7–8 Ungrouted sun face.

Prepare the Base

1. Many sun bases have deep insets or raised areas for the sun's facial features. They also have ridges for the sun's rays. To even them out, apply a coating of thinset cement with protective gloves. This makes it easier to apply the tesserae over the surface. Allow the cement to cure overnight.

Apply the Features

2. Following the shapes on the base, use a pencil to draw guidelines for the eyes, eyebrows, and lips. Use the side biters to cut the red-orange tiles into shapes that will fill in the lips and eyebrows. Cut a blue circle and two white triangles for each eye. Apply thinset cement with a palette knife to adhere each piece. Butter the back of each piece and press firmly onto the base (Photo 7–6). As an alternative, apply cement to the base and press each piece into it firmly. Use the dental pick to clean off any excess cement that may have squished out. This allows you to place the next piece up close without having to chisel away at the excess.

Create the Face

3. Put on safety glasses. Use the scorer/breaker to cut the yellow-gold tiles in half. This makes them a more manageable size for nipping. I like to lay one side of the face first and pay special attention to the shape of the tesserae (Photo 7–7). Notice the dimples, the angles of the nose, etc. Then I create the other side to match. This gives the face a symmetry and evenness.

Add Sun's Rays

4. After finishing the face, a single row of burnt-orange tesserae finishes it off by giving definition and a starting point to the rays. I chose to make the rays out of long angular shapes to emphasize the outward points (Photo 7–8).

Grouting

5. Grout as per instructions on pages 112–115. I chose terra-cotta-color grout so it would blend with the terra-cotta form underneath. After the grout has fully cured, seal with a penetrating grout sealer.

Finished front.

Finished back.

TIME-OUT CHAIR

LEVEL: ADVANCED

Furniture is a fun base for mosaics. Many mosaicists use recycled china and old furniture to create pieces in the "shabby chic" style. This child's chair is intended to make sitting in the corner a little more fun. The clock and other symbols are a graphic reinforcement of the chair's purpose.

MATERIALS

• Plain wooden chair, child's size
• 2-inch (5-cm) matte ceramic tiles in white and black
• 1-inch (2.5-cm) matte ceramic tiles in pink, purple, blue
• PVA glue (like WeldBond)
• Black sanded grout
• Penetrating grout sealer

TOOLS

• Side biter nippers
• Pro scorer/breaker
• 2-inch (5-cm) sponge brush
• Pencil and permanent marker
• Dental tool
• Grout sponge
• Safety glasses

Prepare the Base

1. Seal all the exposed surfaces by painting with a sealing mixture of one-part PVA glue and four-parts water. After the sealer has dried, use a pencil to draw in the clock, symbols, and words "Time Out." Then use a permanent marker to darken the lines.

7–9 Apply the clock face to the seat. Use a dental tool to clean excess glue.

7–10 Establish the pattern for the sides of the chair.

Apply the Motifs

2. Put on safety glasses. Use the scorer/breaker to cut the black tiles in half. This makes it a more manageable size for nipping. Use the nippers to cut the hands, time markers, and rim of the clock. Following the guidelines that you drew, apply the tesserae to the seat with the glue.

7–11 Finish the sides and then begin filling in the white background on the seat.

7–12 Ungrouted front of chair.

Use the dental pick to clean off any excess glue that may have squished out (Photo 7–9). This allows you to set the adjacent piece up close.

Start at the Legs

3. After the clock is dry, lay the chair on its back. The idea is to mosaic the entire side of one surface at a time and then turn the chair to a second side after the glue dries. Lay the blue tiles like diamonds, point to point, along the legs and the sides of the back. Adjust the spacing and glue all the blue tiles down. Score and break a lot of the black and white tiles in half. Then use the nippers to break the halves one more time to create quarters. Cut each quarter diagonally to create two triangles. Alternate black and white triangles between the blue diamonds (Photo 7–10).

4. Cut some of the purple and pink tiles in half vertically. Some of these will be cut down into

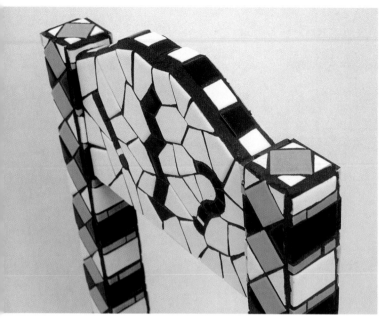

7–13 Top of sides and slats.

7–14 Finished seat.

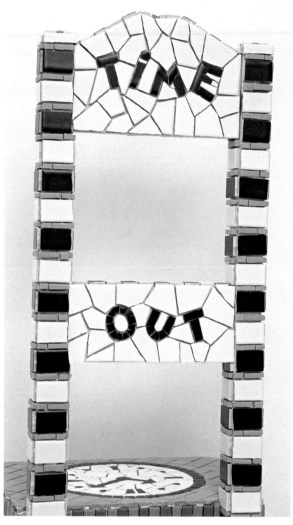

7–15 Ungrouted back of chair.

7–16 Pattern on the seat edge and supports.

Kathryn Luther. *Hot Seat*, 2000. 44 x 19 x 16 inches
(112 x 48 x 41 cm). Handmade ceramic. Photo by the artist.

Steve and **Zoe Terlizzese.** *"Love Lives Here" Hall Tree*, 2001.
74 x 26 x 16 inches (188 x 66 x 41 cm). Wood, tile, china, game
piece, tapestry fabric, pottery, mirror. Photo by Lynn Johnson.

Left: **Sonia King.** *Flying Colors*, 2001. 6.8 x 5 x 31.5 feet (2.1 x 1.5 x 9.6 m). Marble gems, mirror. Photo by Sheila Cunningham.

Below: **Shug Jones** and **Lynne Chinn.** *El Lagartijo*, 2001. 36 x 48 inches (91 x 122 cm). Vitreous glass, art glass. Photo by the artist.

Above: **Jude Schlotzhauer.** *Fish de Verre*, 2001. 34 x 66 x 18 inches (86 x 168 x 46 cm). Glass fusions, glass. Photo by Taylor Dabney.

Left: **Bruce** and **Shannon Anderson.** *Untitled*, 2001. 41 x 41 x 21 inches (104 x 104 x 53 cm). Stoneware. Photo by the artist.

Lillian Sizemore and Laurel True. *Mission Creek Mural*, 1999. 8.5 x 15 feet (2.6 x 4.6 m). Ceramic, mirror, gold tile. Photo by Alon Picker.

Lillian Sizemore and Laurel True. *Mission Creek Mural* (detail), 1999. 8.5 x 15 feet (2.6 x 4.6 m). Ceramic, mirror, gold tile. Photo by Alon Picker.

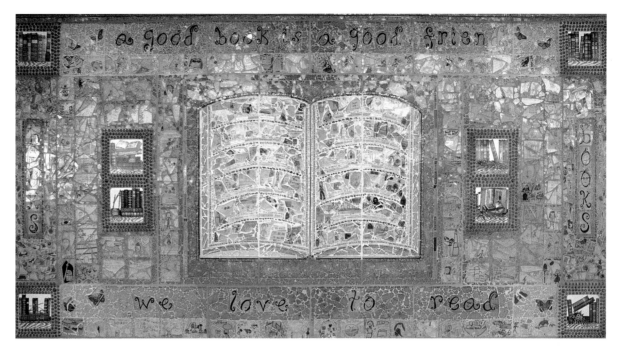

Ellen Blakely. *A Good Book*, 2000. 6 x 12 feet (1.8 x 3.7 m). Glass, marble gems, ceramic, found objects. San Francisco, CA. Photo by the artist.

Ellen Blakely. *A Good Book* (detail), 2000. 6 x 12 feet (1.8 x 3.7 m). Glass, marble gems, ceramic, found objects. San Francisco, CA. Photo by the artist.

Angela Casazza. *Cornucopia*, 1996. 24 x 12 inches (61 x 31 cm). China, hand-painted tiles, ceramic. Photo by the artist.

Elizabeth Mahassine. *Funerary Urn*, 1999. 7 x 4-inch (18 x 10-cm) diameter. Glass. Photo by Debra St. John.

Cynthia Reynolds. *Vessel*, 1994. 20 x 14 inches (51 x 36 cm). Ceramic. Photo by the artist.

Carolina Zanelli. *My Shower*, 2001 2.3 x 3 x 6.6 feet
(70 x 90 x 200 cm). Tiles, cups. Photo by Marco Ciairo.

Top Right: **Robert Bellamy.** *Lucy Reeves Memory Fireplace.* Childhood keepsakes, pottery, jewelry. Photo by the artist.

Below Left: **Elizabeth Mahassine.** *Jones Mosaic Dome Ceiling*, 1998. 2 x 8-feet (60 cm x 2.4-m) diameter. Glass, dichroic glass, fiber optics. Photo by Ian Tervet.

Below Right: **Tessa Hunkin.** *Vegetables*, 2000. 5 x 10 feet (1.5 x 3 m). Vitreous glass. Photo by the artist.

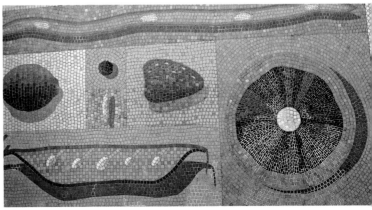

Noelle M. Horsefield. *Three Cats*, 2001. 36 x 24 inches
(91 x 61 cm). Smalti. Photo by the artist.

George Fishman. *Moonlight Winter Birches*, 2001. 60 x 48 inches
(152 x 122 cm). Stone, smalti. Photo by the artist.

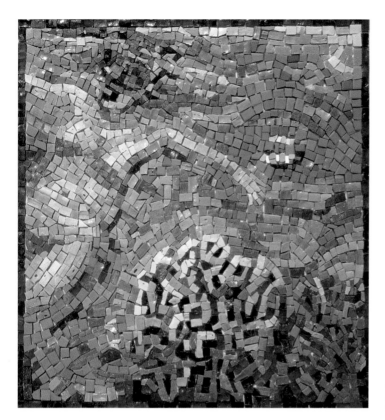

Left: **George Fishman.** *Snorkeling*, 2000. 18 x 18 inches (46 x 46 cm). Smalti, marble. Photo by the artist.

Above: **Sarah Zirkel.** *Gilding the Lily*, 2001. 22.25-inch (56.5-cm) diameter. Smalti, marble. Photo by Rob Buck.

Left: **George Fishman.** *Tropical Bouquet*, 2000. 4 x 3 feet (1.2 x .9 m). Smalti, golds. Photo by the artist.

Above: **Carlos Cohen.** *La Marseillaise*, 1976. 9.2 x 7.5 feet (2.8 x 2.3 m). Smalti. Photo by the artist.

Top Right: **Irina Charny.** *Mariposa*, 2003. 28 x 37 inches (71 x 94 cm). Glass, glazed and unglazed porcelain, beads, china, millefiori, gold, pyrite. Photo by Ben Charny.

Bottom Right: **Jason Cohen.** *Tigers.* 29 x 23 inches (74 x 58 cm). Stained glass. Photo By Brian West.

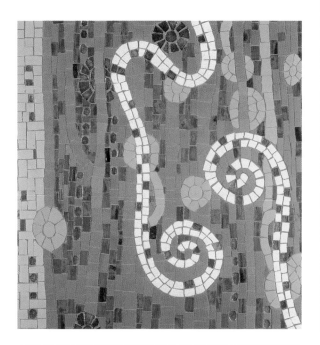

Top Left: **Sherri King.** *Emotions*, 2001. 18 x 18 inches (46 x 46 cm). Ceramic, vitreous glass, golds. Photo by author.

Top Right: **Diana Maria Rossi.** *"A Little Bit of Beauty to Remember #3 (for us, for George),"* 1999. 5.75 x 13.5 x 4.75 inches (15 x 34 x 12 cm). Glass mosaic with text. Photo by the artist.

Above: **Laura Bradley.** *The Eastern Gate*, 1991. 22 x 4 x 3 inches (56 x 10 x 8 cm). Marble, stone, bronze, ceramic, copper. Photo by the artist.

Mireille Levesque. *La Femme Hibou*, 1998. 6 x 2 feet (1.8 m x 60 cm). Ceramic, vitreous glass. Photo by Catherine LeBlanc.

Sonia King. *Odyssey*, 2002. 26 x 19 inches (66 x 48 cm). Slate, ceramic, glass, aluminum, smalti, millefiore, pebbles. Photo by Expert Imaging.

Right: **Jerry Carter.** *Apertura*, 1987. 23 x 34 inches (58 x 86 cm). Smalti, marble, etched glass, golds. Photo by the artist.

Below: **Val Carroll. H.** *Serendipidus VI*, 1994. 33 inch x 7.6 feet x 5 inches (84 cm x 2.3 m x 13 cm). Glass. Photo by the artist.

Norman Tellis. *Flora*, 2000. 30 x 24 inches (76 x 61 cm). Smalti, vitreous glass, crackle glass, glass cabochons. Photo by the artist.

Boline Strand. *Fredrik*, 2001. 11.25 x 11.25 inches (28.6 x 28.6 cm). Smalti, marble. Photo by John Ramirez.

Opposite Page: **Ken Knowlton.** *"I Shall Never Believe that God Plays Dice with the World"* — *Albert Einstein*, 1999. 33 x 27 inches (84 x 69 cm). Dice. Photo by the artist.

Karla Cinquanta. *Hillary Clinton: Into Her Own*, 2000. 5.2 x 3.2 feet (1.6 m x 98 cm). Glazed and unglazed ceramic, vitreous glass, gold-leaf tesserae. Photo by David Caras Photography.

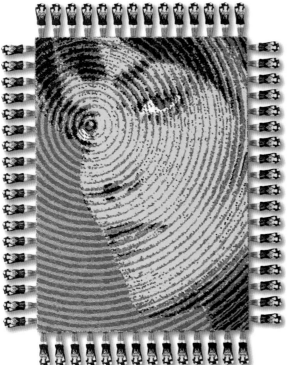

Artboy. *Bead Zena*, 1999. 40 x 32 inches (102 x 81 cm). Around 44,000 glass beads, crystals, and Xena toys on wood. Photo by the artist.

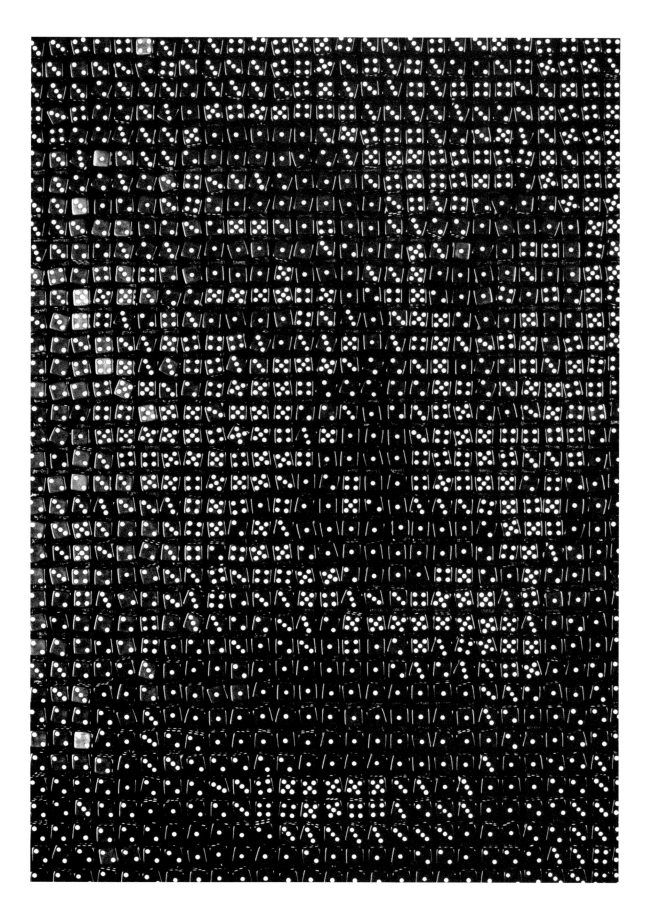

Opposite Page, Top Left: **David B. Hickman.** *Virgin of Guadalupe*, 2001. Fused glass, copper. Photo by the artist.

Opposite Page, Right: **George Fishman.** *Faces of Flower Avenue*, 1991. 9.5 x 3-feet (2.9 m x 90-cm) diameter. Ceramic, glass. Photo by the artist.

Opposite Page, Bottom Left: **Lia Catalano.** *Apollo*, 2000. 12-inch (31-cm) diameter. Vitreous glass, golds. Photo by the artist.

Left: **Gay McCarter.** *Jackson and the Arts* (detail), 2000. 21 x 5 feet (6.4 x 1.5 m). Ceramic. Photo by the artist.

Below: **Isaiah Zagar.** *609 South Alder Street*, 1996. Mirror and ceramic tile. Philadelphia, PA. Photo by the artist.

Opposite Page: **Niki Glen** and **Helen Helwig.** Butterfly Garden Bench (detail), 1999. 5 x 3 feet (1.5 x .9 m). Handmade clay mosaics. Photo by the artist.

Right: **Susan Tunnick.** *Brighton Clay Re-Leaf #1* (detail), 1994. 8 x 40 feet (2.4 x .12 m). Ceramic. Prospect Park Subway Station, Brooklyn, NY. Photo by Peter Mauss/Esto.

Below: **Niki Glen** and **Helen Helwig.** *"Our Community"* Sidewalk Mosaic, 2000. 4 x 4 feet (1.2 x 1.2 m). Handmade clay mosaics. Photo by the artist.

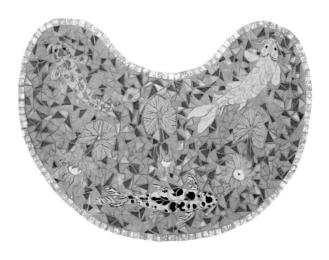

Right: **Jennifer** and **Bobby Parker.** *Koi Fish Pond.* 36 x 24 inches (91 x 61 cm). Handmade tile. Photo by the artist.

Left: **Robert Stout.** *The Pathway II*, 1993. 5 x 35 feet (1.5 x 10.7 m). Photo by the artist.

Right: **Mesolini Glass Studio.** *Bainbridge Islands Beach Glass Quilt*, 1999. 10 x 10 feet (3 x 3 m). Beach glass, fused glass, polished rocks. Photo by Greg Gilbert.

Below: **Gay McCarter.** *Swimming Koi*, 1999. 2 x 3 feet (60 x 90 cm). Vitreous glass. Photo by the artist.

Lili Ann Killian Rosenberg. *Forest* (detail), 1988. 6 x 12 feet (1.8 x 3.7 m). Ceramic, stone, glass, found objects, concrete. Photo by the artist.

Lili Ann Killian Rosenberg. *Celebrate Children*, 1989. 18 x 36 feet (5.5 x 11 m). Ceramic, glass, found objects and concretes. St. Christopher's Children's Hospital, Philadelphia, PA. Photo by the artist.

Marcelo de Melo. *34 double T*, 2000. 22 x 12 x 4 inches (55 x 30 x 10 cm). China, coconut shells. Photo by Paola Lazcano.

Wendy Grossman de Segovia. *Pandas and Cows*. China, ceramic, glass. Photo by the artist.

Above: **Judy Barnett.** *Snake Table*, 1999. 22 x 31 inches (56 x 78 cm). Vitreous glass. Photo by the artist.

Right: **Timmerman Daugherty.** *Just Ducky*, 2000. Stained glass, marbles, pottery, found objects. Photo by John Lehr.

8–4 Finished close-up.

7. Use uncut gold tiles to edge the border. They should fit perfectly outside the pencil guide marks you made at the beginning. It will be necessary to cut a few pieces into angles in order to fit them above and below the beginning of the swirl (Photo 8–3).

Grouting

8. Grout as per instructions on pages 112–115. I chose a brown-colored grout to enhance the golds and greens and make the swirl easier to follow (Photo 8–4). A black grout would be too severe while a light-colored grout would fracture the look.

SITES TO SEE

Australia	Melbourne	Metropolitan Fire Brigade
	Sydney	Skygarden
	Brisbane	International Airport
	Geelong	Victoria State Government Office
	Perth	Train Station
China	Beijing	Forbidden City
	Hong Kong	Hong Kong Bank
Japan	Tokyo	Koriyama Station
	Kanagawa	Cultural Center
New Zealand	Auckland	Marsden Wharf
	Kawakawa	Public Toilets (by Hundertwasser)

SUN DISKS

Level: Intermediate

Hang these sparkling disks in the garden to capture the sun. Although these disks are made of mirror tiles, you can make them with other materials, such as stained glass, marble gems, and beach glass.

Materials
- Cookie-tin lids in three sizes
- Thinset cement mortar with admix
- Two-part epoxy, quick-setting
- Mirror tiles
- Black sanded grout
- Penetrating grout sealer

Tools
- Glass scorer
- Running pliers
- Wheeled cutters
- Metal ruler
- A few toothpicks

- Palette knife
- Craft sticks
- Dental tool
- Grout sponge
- Hammer and nail
- Safety glasses
- Gloves
- Nylon filament

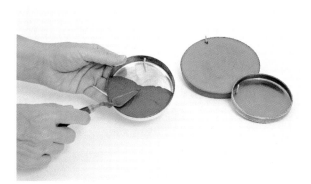

8–5 Fill cookie tin lids with cement. Note the toothpick protecting the hole.

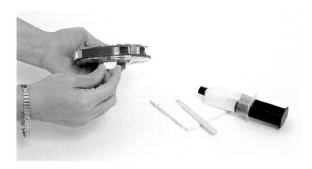

8–6 Apply mirror to the rim with epoxy and craft stick.

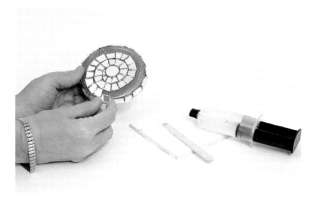

8–7 Apply patterns.

8–8 Tie filament through the holes for hanging.

Prepare the Bases

1. Use the hammer and nail to punch a small hole near the edge of each lid. This provides a hole for you to hang the disk.

2. Insert a toothpick into the hole and leave about a ¼ inch (6 mm) extended past both sides of the lid. Use the palette knife to fill each lid with cement (Photo 8–5). Allow to dry overnight.

Creating and Applying the Mirror Tiles

3. Use the scoring tool and running pliers to create mirrored tesserae. The wheeled cutters are handy for trimming shapes. I chose three different patterns for my lids: a swirl, wave, and chevron motif. Feel free to create your own pattern. Start by applying the tiles around the rims of the lids with the quick-setting epoxy and a craft stick (Photo 8–6).

4. Decide how you want to place the tesserae on the lids. When working with quick-setting epoxy, there isn't much time to change your mind, so be ready once the epoxy is mixed (Photo 8–7). Mix a small batch at a time, as it quickly becomes unusable. Apply it with a craft stick. Be sure to leave the toothpick and its hole exposed for hanging later.

NOTE: *Some epoxies have a very strong odor. Always work in a well-ventilated area. You may even consider using a respirator. If you're prone to getting adhesive on your skin, wear thin gloves while working.*

Grouting

5. Grout as per instructions on pages 112–115. I chose a black grout to emphasize the reflective mirror and make the pieces more dramatic.

Sealing and Finishing

6. After the grout has fully cured, seal with a penetrating grout sealer.

7. Twist and pull out the toothpicks. You may need a pair of pliers to do this. Use fishing line filament to create invisible hangers (Photo 8–8).

SITES TO SEE NEAR THE MIDDLE EAST

Algeria	Algiers	Algiers Museum
	Cherchel	Roman Mosaics
	Djemila	House of Bacchus
	Lambese	Musée Municipal
	Timgad	Timgad Museum
Egypt	Alexandria	Graeco-Roman Museum, Archeological Park
	Cairo	St. Mary Coptic Church, National Museum
	Mt. Sinai	Monastery of St. Catherine
Israel	Bethlehem	Church of the Nativity
	Beth Alpha	Synagogue
	Gaza	Synagogue
	Hammath Tiberius	Roman Spa
	Jerusalem	The Knesset (by Marc Chagall), Armenian Church, Dome of the Rock, Mosque El Aksa
Jordan	Jerash	Museum and various sites
	Jericho	Hisham Palace, Khirbet-el-Mafjar
	Madaba	Byzantine Church, Map of Madaba, Archeological Park and Mosaic School, Archeological Museum, Hippolytus Hall
	Mount Nebo	Museum and various sites
	Qasr al-Hallabat	Umayyad Castle
Lebanon	Baalbek	Palace of Diocletian Spaleto
	Beirut	Beit el Din Palace, Helix Fountain (by Marco Bravura)
Libya	Zliten	Roman Villa
Morocco		Site of Volubilis
Oman	Muscat	Mosque of the Golden Dome
Syria	Damascus	Mosque of Omayyads, Baybars' Mausoleum, Mausoleum of Tankiz, Damascus Museum, The Great Mosque
Tunisia	Bulla Regia	House of the Hunt
	Carthage	Musée de Carthage, Parc des Thérmès d'Antonia, Villa des Volières
	El-Jem	Musée d' El-Jem
	Sfax	Archeological Museum
	Sousse	Archeological Museum, Musée de Sousse
	Tunis	Bardo Museum
	Utique	Antiquarium d' Utique

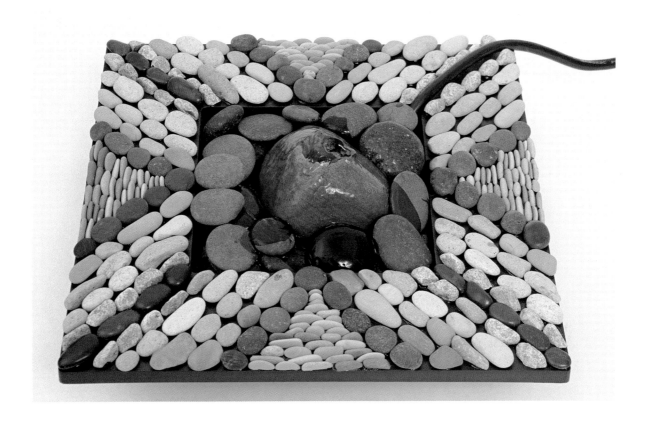

ROCK GARDEN FOUNTAIN

LEVEL: INTERMEDIATE

The East inspires visions of rock gardens and water features. The sound of running water creates a serene setting for relaxing after a busy day. Pebbles are a natural choice for creating fountains. No grouting is necessary on this project.

MATERIALS
• Hard plastic fountain base with a wide, flat rim
• Variety of small colored pebbles (black, gray, pink, turquoise)
• Pump
• Large pebbles for fountain center

TOOLS
• Side biter nippers
• Two-part epoxy, quick-setting
• Craft sticks
• Tweezers
• Safety glasses
• Gloves

Create the Design

1. Play around with the materials until you find a pattern that pleases you (Photo 8–9). I decided to work with diagonals. Laying longer pebbles end to end establishes some *andamento* even in this limited space. One of the concerns with a tabletop fountain is what to do with the electrical cord. I decided to solve the problem by laying a line of shiny black pebbles on three of the four corners. The fourth corner allows the cord to lay between two rows of pink pebbles (Photo 8–10).

8–9 Work with the pebbles to find a pleasing pattern.

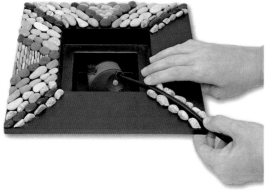

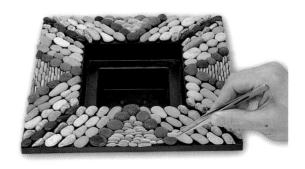

8–10 Before gluing, make sure that the cord fits in the groove between the pebbles in one corner. Remove the pump while finishing the project.

8–11 Set the thin pebble halves on edge with tweezers.

Apply the Pebbles

2. Mix a small batch of epoxy at a time, as it will quickly become unusable. Apply it with a craft stick. When working with quick-setting epoxy, there isn't much time to change your mind, so be ready to place the tesserae once the epoxy is mixed.

NOTE: *Some epoxies have a very strong odor. Always work in a well-ventilated area. You may even consider using a respirator. If you're prone to getting adhesive on your skin, wear thin gloves while working.*

3. Set aside any thin flat pebbles. Put on safety glasses. Use the nippers and cut these in half lengthwise. Then set them on the fountain's edge to add a different texture to the inner triangle (Photo 8–11). Leave the fountain ungrouted in order to add to the textural effect.

Assemble the Fountain

4. Follow the pump manufacturer's instructions for setting up the fountain. Most small pumps have an adjustable water flow. Be sure that yours isn't set too high or else water will splash out of the fountain. Run the cord out along the space that was left in one corner.

SITES TO SEE

India	Chandigarh	The Rock Garden
Russia	St. Petersburg	Cathedral of St. Isaac, The Hermitage
Turkey	Antakya	Mosaic Museum, Hatay Archeological Museum, Villa of Constantine
	Ephesus	Museum and ruins
	Istanbul	Kariye Camii, Archeological Museum, Fethiye Camii, Hagia Sophia, Great Palace Mosaic Museum
Ukraine	Pochaev	Pochaev Monastery
	Kiev	Santa Sophia

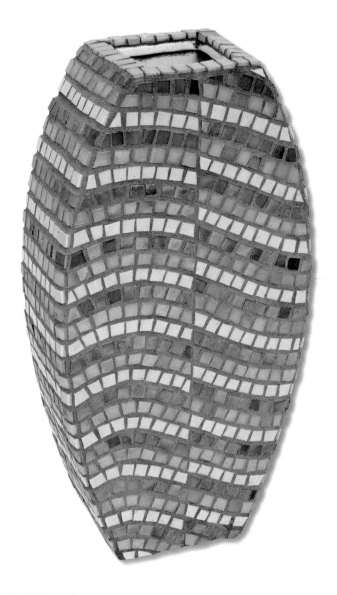

ISLAND WAVE VASE

LEVEL: ADVANCED

Here's a project that's inspired by breaking waves of the South Pacific islands. Three colors of turquoise tiles combine for a sense of movement and rhythm. The vertical break and slipping of the pattern adds interest and tension. Experiment with various curves and shapes till you find one that pleases you.

MATERIALS
- Ceramic vase
- Three colors of turquoise glass tiles, two iridescent and one plain
- Medium-blue sanded grout
- PVA glue (WeldBond)

TOOLS
- Coarse sandpaper
- Wheeled cutters
- Ruler
- Permanent marker
- Tweezers
- Dental tool
- Grout sponge
- Safety glasses

8-12 Choose a range of colors. Draw your template onto the vase.

Prepare the Base

1. Use coarse sandpaper on the outside of the vase to roughen the surface for better adhesion.

2. Cut a wave template out of a piece of cardboard or paper. Lay the template across the sides of the vase and use the marker to draw guidelines (Photo 8–12). These lines may not align exactly with your tesserae but they will give you an indication if you are going off track. Continue the lines to the other side and draw more waves.

NOTE: *If your tiles are translucent, don't use a black marker. The guidelines may show through.*

3. Use a ruler to draw a vertical line down the center of each side. This line will allow you to create the illusion of movement by "sliding" the pattern down.

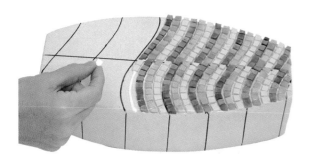

8-13 Apply the colors on the first side. Shift one row along the center line.

Start the Pattern

4. Use the wheeled cutters to create an inventory of quartered tiles in each color. Keep the colors separate. It helps prevent confusion to lay the colors out in the same order as your pattern.

5. Lay the vase on its side and start working from one end to the other. Lay the tesserae in rows of dark, medium, light on the left side and medium, light, dark on the right (Photo 8–13). Keep repeating the pattern until the side is done. Use the dental pick to clean any glue that may prevent the grout from filling the joints. Allow the side to dry overnight.

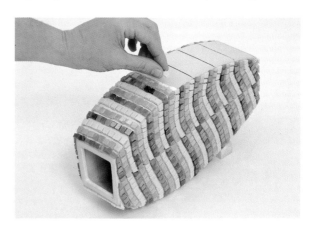

8-14 Continue onto the side. A support under the vase keeps the top level.

8-15 Finished vase, ungrouted.

Continue the Pattern

6. Continue the rows around the first side (Photo 8–14), allow to dry, and then repeat the wave on the back. Finally, connect the front and back across the last side. Because of the vase's curved sides, you may need to use a support to keep a level working surface. After drying, lay quarter tiles around the top edge (Photo 8–15).

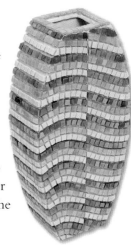

Grout

7. Grout as per instructions on pages 112–115. I chose a medium-blue colored grout to enhance the pattern.

THE CHAPERONE

LEVEL: ADVANCED

Nek Chand created a world of mosaic people and figures called *The Rock Garden* in Chandigarh, India. Like Raymond Isidore in France, Chand uses broken china and recycled materials. He created this huge visionary space in solitude at night after working all the day as a transport official. This project illustrates how to create three-dimensional sculptures from readily available materials. While this figure is done entirely in white, you can create a variety of characters using colored tile and china.

MATERIALS
- 20-inch (51-cm) Styrofoam cone
- 6-inch (15-cm) diameter Styrofoam ball
- 10-inch (25-cm) wooden dowel and toothpicks
- PVA glue (WeldBond)
- Thinset cement mortar with admix

- An assortment of white ceramic tiles: shiny, matte, textured, round, and square
- A variety of white cup and mug handles
- White sanded grout
- Penetrating grout sealer

TOOLS
- Serrated knife
- Side biter nippers
- Pro scorer/breaker
- Palette knife
- Dental tool
- Grout sponge
- Safety glasses
- Gloves

8–16 Cut pieces being assembled.

8–17 Coat form with thinset.

Prepare the Base

1. Using a serrated knife, cut the top third of the Styrofoam cone off. Then vertically cut this top-third section in half. These halves will be the two arms and hands. Carve each half into a rough approximation of an arm and hand.

2. Poke the dowel halfway into the top of the base and halfway into the ball. Fill each hole with glue. Squeeze a little extra glue into the top of the base. Insert the dowel into the base and push the ball onto the exposed part of the dowel (Photo 8–16). Press the ball and base together firmly.

3. Insert a toothpick into each side of the body where the arms will be attached. Apply some glue and then attach the arms/hands. Allow to dry overnight.

Finish the Base

4. Wearing protective gloves, apply a coating of thinset cement over the form (Photo 8–17). This will give you a strong surface to adhere the mosaic.

8–18 Apply the jacket with thinset.

8–19 Finish jacket body, then create the sleeves.

8–20 Start pattern on skirt.

If the form is very large, wrap the Styrofoam in wire mesh first before you apply the thinset. This will give added strength to the structure. Allow cement to cure overnight.

Organize the Tiles

5. Decide which tiles you would like to use for the different parts of the form. You'll notice there are slight variations in the whites of different tiles. Save the matte-textured tiles for the skin tone of the face and hands. Choose another set as the material of the jacket, several for the pattern of the skirt, one for hair, and so on.

Jacket

6. Cut the larger ceramic tiles in half using the scorer/breaker. Use nippers to shape two triangles for the points of the collar. Create rectangles to go around the waist. If you don't have any small round tiles, you can either cut circles or use real buttons on the jacket.

7. Use thinset to apply the jacket features. Use rectangles to define the waistband (Photo 8–18). Finish the jacket using a crazy-paving pattern (Photo 8–19).

Skirt

8. Use the rectangles to do the hem, then fill in the rest of the skirt. Depending on the tiles available, you can create your own pattern or follow the one shown in Photo 8–20. I first applied long, narrow

8–21 Use side biters to trim the cup and mug handles for the nose and ears.

tiles from the waistband to the hem. Then I connected those with diagonals, alternating one tile up and one tile down Finally, fill in the open panes of the skirt.

Face and Hands
9. Trim the cup handles to define the lips, nose, and eyebrows (Photo 8–21). Use the mug handles to make the ears. Small handles can make earrings. A circle and two triangles make each eye. Finish off the hair by leaving a wide grout line on one side for a part. Use long, narrow tiles to create the hair. Lay the tiles from the top of the head to the bottom. For each hand, place a large piece for the back, then lay the thumb and each finger separately (Photos 8–22 and 8–23).

Grouting
10. Grout as per instructions on pages 112–115. I chose a white grout to pull the entire form together as well as to emphasize the severity and mysterious air of the work. A darker grout would accent the cutting and laying more.

Sealing
11. After the grout has fully cured, seal with a penetrating grout sealer.

8–22 Define the features on the face. Apply the tesserae to the hands.

8–23 Finished, but ungrouted.

Above: **Melbourne Mural Studio.** *Milky Way Dreaming* (being created), 1991. 25 x 25 feet (7.5 x 7.5 m). Smalti. Photo by David Jack.

Left: **Melbourne Mural Studio.** *Works in Progress,* 1992. Photo by David Jack.

Opposite Page: **Hashimura Motohiro.**
Mural: Cultural Center. Smalti.
Kanagawa, Japan. Photo by the artist.

Above: **Hashimura Motohiro.**
Mural: Yamanashi Culture Center.
Marble, smalti. Photo by the artist.

Left: **Miyauchi Junkichi.** Exterior of a
Coffeehouse. Photo by the artist.

Following Pages: **Harold Freeman.**
The Legends of Football (detail),
1986. Photo by David Jack.

Above: **Ilana Shafir.** *Ripples of Creation*, 2001. 7.9 x 5.5 feet (2.4 x 1.7 m). Stones, shells, coral, handmade ceramics, gold, found objects, glass. Photo by the artist.

Opposite Page: **Ilana Shafir.** *Cosmic Streams*, 2001. 3.3 x 4.1 feet (1 x 1.25 m). Stone, smalti, handmade ceramic, shells, coral, found objects, pebbles. Photo by the artist.

Robert Preston (designer). *The Mixing of Memory with Desire*,
1994. 8.2 x 31.2 feet (2.5 x 9.5 m). Brisbane, Australia. Photo courtesy
of Brisbane International Airport.

Above: **Suzanne Garrard.** *Majorca Outdoor Dining Table*, 1997. 7.9
x 3.3 feet (2.4 x 1 m). Vitreous. Photo by Chris Greenhout.

Opposite Page: **Suzanne Garrard.** *By the Brook Fountain Wall*, 1998.
10.8 square yards (9 sq m). Pebbles. Photo by Shannon McGrath.

Top: **Kate Millington.** *Native Flora of Grey Lynn (detail Pohutakawa)*, 2001. 2 x 30 feet (60 cm x 9 m). Ceramic. Auckland, New Zealand. Photo by Jo Clarke.

Bottom: **Elaine Prunty.** Baker Mosaic Puzzle, 1998. 3.3 x 8 feet (1 x 2.5 m). Colored, iridescent, and textured stained glass. Photo by the artist.

Top: **Sandra Robertson.** *View from Queenslander Deck*, 2001. Ceramic, metal, driftwood, found objects, glass. Photo by the artist.

Above: **Kate Rattray.** *Birch Leaf Paving Stone*, 1995. 17 x 13 x 1.6 inches (44 x 34 x 4 cm). Mirror. Photo by Ian Dart.

Right: **Sandra Robertson.** *Anyone for Opera? Sydney Style*, 2001. 35 x 24 inches (90 x 60 cm). Tiles, stones, glass, earrings, twigs. Photo by the artist.

Top Left: **Rebecca Wilkie Designs.** *Calypso Sun*, 2001. 4 square yards (3.3 sq m). Vitreous glass and golds. Photo by the artist.

Top Right: **Michelle Freeman.** *Paua Tranquil Fountain*, 2000. 5 x 2.6 feet (1.5 m x 80 cm). Ceramic and vitreous glass. Photo by Chris Vile.

Right: **Rebecca Wilkie Designs.** *Our New World*, 2000. 3.3 x 6.6 feet (1 x 2 m). Ceramic and golds. Photo by the artist.

Following Pages: **Maggy Howarth.** *Dancing Fishes Fountain* (detail), 2000. Pebbles and slate. Photo by the artist.

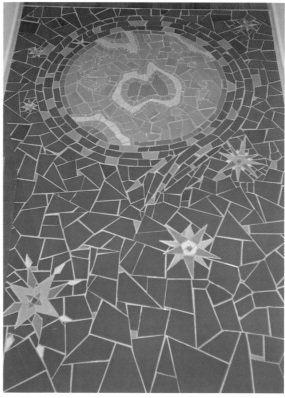

GLOSSARY

Admix (or admixture): A latex additive for thinset cement that increases flexibility and durability. Some cement-based adhesives have a dry additive already in the mix.

Andamento: Italian for "trend" or "course." The rhythm and flow of a mosaic created by controlling the lines between rows of tiles.

Backbiting: Using the flat, or backside, of the nippers to cut the tiles.

Cartoon: A full-size design drawing for a mosaic.

Cement-based adhesive: *See* Thinset.

Direct method: A technique in which the tesserae are fixed directly onto a base with an adhesive.

Emblema (pl. emblemata): A mosaic inset, or panel, set into floor mosaics. It is usually surrounded by a border or geometric pattern.
Filati: Threads of enameled glass used in micro-

mosaics. They are placed on end in adhesive and cut to the correct depth.

Frost-proof: Tile or mosaic material that will withstand extremes of temperature and exposure to weather.

Grout: Cement-based mixture used to fill the joints between tiles and protect the surface from dirt and moisture. Not an adhesive.

Grout river: The line created when the joints between tiles align. It may be intended or unintended.

Hammer and hardie: A heavy, sharp hammer and matching chisel head usually set into a log. Used for cutting tesserae.

Indirect method (or reverse method): A technique in which the design is first created backwards and then reversed at installation. The tesserae are placed facedown using temporary adhesive on a temporary mounting surface. The

Opposite Page: View from the Office of Angelo Orsoni Srl, Venice. Photo by author.

mosaic is then flipped over onto a permanent adhesive and base.

Interstice: The space or joint between tesserae.

Keystoning: A technique for cutting the tesserae to fit smoothly around a curve.

Mastic: A paste-like adhesive for tiles in interior use with limited water exposure.

Nibbling: Using the center part of the nipper jaws to cut tiles.

Nipping: Creating a controlled fracture in a tile in order to cut it into the desired shape. This is done with the protruding side of the nippers.

***Opus* (pl. *opera*):** Latin word for a "creative work." Refers to the way in which a mosaic is worked or laid.

Opus circumactum: A technique for laying the tesserae in a repeating fan-shaped pattern.

Opus musivum: *Opus vermiculatum* used over the entire surface of a mosaic, radiating outward.

Opus palladianum: A technique in which random-shaped tesserae are laid in a random manner. This is also known as crazy paving.

Opus regulatum: A technique in which the tesserae laid in a pattern like a grid or graph paper. The vertical and horizontal grout lines align.

Opus sectile: A technique in which a single section or tessera of material defines an element of the design.

Opus tesselatum: A technique in which the tesserae are laid in a brick-laying pattern. The horizontal grout lines are aligned while the vertical lines are offset.

Opus vermiculatum: A technique in which the tesserae are laid in a worm-like, winding manner often outlining a shape.

Picassiette: Literally meaning "plate stealer," it is a term used to describe broken china mosaics.

Polychrome: Having many colors.

PVA (polyvinyl acetate): A water-soluble white glue that is odorless, non-toxic, and dries clear.

Retemper: To add liquid to grout or cement-based adhesive after initial mixing. This weakens the final product.

Reverse method: *See* indirect method.

Riven edge: The rough, broken edge of a tessera (usually marble or stone).

Scoring: Creating a precise scratch across the surface of a tile before snapping it.

Side biters: Most commonly used tile nippers.

Slake: To allow the grout to begin its chemical process.

Smalti: An enameled glass that was used by the Byzantines. They come in a large range of colors. They are usually hand cut and highly light refractive.

Thinset: A sticky, fine-grained, and waterproof cement-based adhesive. Also called mortar.

Vitreous glass tile: A pressed-glass mosaic tile with a beveled edge.

SUPPLIERS/RESOURCES

In order to provide you with the most up-to-date information, please visit http://www.mosaicartist. com, where the suppliers' listing is updated frequently. Click on "Links." You'll find numerous companies listed with their Web address and/or mailing address and phone number. Additional information includes links to mosaic associations and information resources.

RECOMMENDED READING

Please refer to the above website to also find a recommended reading list of mosaic books. Many are available in bookstores today. Some are out of print, but it is well worth the effort to search for them in used bookstores or on the Internet.

CONTRIBUTING ARTISTS

Bruce and Shannon Kelly Andersen, Andersen Studios, Seattle, WA, USA

Artboy, Rosemead, CA, USA

Monica Rossella Baccolini Pisilli, Alfonsine, Italy

Candace Bahouth, Pilton, Somerset, UK

Judy Barnett, Brockenhurst, Hants, UK

Robert Bellamy, Reptile, Dallas, TX, USA

Emma Biggs, Mosaic Workshop, London, UK

Ilaria Bison, Udine, Italy

Ellen Blakely, San Francisco, CA, USA

Diane Bonciolini, Mesolini Glass Studio, Bainbridge Island, WA, USA

Laura Bradley, New York, NY, USA

Dusciana Bravura, Ravenna, Italy

Marco Bravura, Ravenna, Italy

Oliver Budd, Goudhurst, Kent, UK

Valerie Carmet, New York, NY, USA

Val M. Carroll, Val Carroll Enterprises Inc., Miami, FL, USA

Jerry Carter, Silver Spring, MD, USA

Angela Casazza, Repsyche Mosaic Art, Sonoma, CA, USA

Lia Catalano, Hannacrois Mosaics, Westerlo, NY, USA

Irina Charny, Irvine, CA, USA

Martin Cheek, Martin Cheek Mosaics, Broadstairs, Kent, UK

Lynne Chinn, Tesserae Mosaic Studio Inc, Plano, TX, USA

Karla Cinquanta, Brookline, MA, USA

Carlos and Jason Cohen, Burbank, CA, USA

Cathie Conzemius, Lone Tree, IA, USA

Eric Rieusset Cros, Palavas Les Flots, France

Sheila Cunningham, Dallas, TX, USA

Carrie Darby, Chalross, Berkshire, UK

Liz d'Ath, London, UK

Timmerman Daugherty, Weirdgardens, Baltimore, MD, USA

Linda Edeiken, Mad Platter Beaded Mosaics, La Jolla, CA, USA

Valeria Ercolani, Ravenna, Italy

Debbie Ernst, Dallas, TX, USA

Robert Field, Farnham, Surrey, UK

George Fishman, George Fishman Mosaics, Miami Shores, FL, USA

Michelle Freeman, Surface Attraction Mosaic Design, Queenstown, New Zealand

Suzanne Garrard, Dargo, Victoria, Australia

Sabina Giuntinelli, Li, Italy

Niki Glen, Southwest Public Art Group, Tempe, AZ, USA

Elaine M. Goodwin, Exeter, UK

Motohiro Hashimura, Yamanasi Tsuru-city, Japan

Helen Helwig, Southwest Public Art Group, Tempe, AZ, USA

David B. Hickman, Dallas, TX, USA

Laura Hiserote, Hiserote Micromosaic, Vancouver, WA, USA

Manfred Hoehn, Munich, Germany

Noelle M. Horsfield, The Smiling Dog Workshop, Huntington, WV, USA

Maggy Howarth, Cobblestone Designs, Lancaster, UK

Sheila Hudson, Eagle, ID, USA

Tessa Hunkin, Mosaic Workshop, London, UK

Sally Imbert, London, UK

Iliev Iliya Ivanov, Sofia, Bulgaria

Shug Jones, Tesserae Mosaic Studio Inc, Plano, TX, USA

Stephanie Jurs, Twin Dolphin Mosaics, Ravenna, Italy

Toyoharu Kii, Tokyo Inagi-city, Japan

Sherri King, Dallas, TX, USA

Sonia King, Sonia King Mosaics, Dallas, TX, USA

Ken Knowlton, Parsippany, NJ, USA

Haruya Kudo, Kudo Haruya Mural Art, Ibaraki-Ken, Japan

Jo Letchford, Canterbury, Kent, UK

Mireille Levesque, Atelier Du Fleure, Varennes, Quebec, Canada

Kathryn Luther, Fargo, ND, USA

Dugald MacInnes, Glasgow, Scotland

Elizabeth Devon Mahassine, San Francisco, CA, USA

Doreen Mastandrea, West Waltham, MA, USA

Gay McCarter, Jackson, TN, USA

Melbourne Mural Studio, Heidelberg West, Victoria, Australia

Marcelo de Melo, Edinburgh, Scotland

Gregg Mesmer, Mesolini Glass Studio, Bainbridge Island, WA, USA

Kate Millington, Auckland, New Zealand

Junkichi Miyauchi, Kanagawa Tuzuki-ku, Japan

Richard Moss, Equipment Of Culture, Holyoke, MA, USA

Jane Muir, Aylesbury, Buckinghamshire, UK

Cleo Mussi, Stroud, Gloucestershire, UK

Wendy Nicholson, Lower Shiplake, Oxfordshire, UK

Felice Nittolo, Ravenna, Italy

Lucio Orsoni, Venice, Italy

Jennifer and Bobby Parker, Juniper Designs, Norfolk, VA, USA

Elaine Prunty, Imago Mosaic, Dublin, Ireland

Eliana Raposo, Atelier Raposo, Sao Paulo, Brazil

Eric Rattan, Santa Fe Design Studio, Madison, WI, USA

Kate Rattray, Over The Moon Mosaics, Wells, Somerset, UK

Rebecca Wilkie Designs, Brisbane, Australia

Cynthia Reynolds, Louisville, KY, USA

Julie Marie Richey, Oggetti Marble Mosaics, Irving, TX, USA

Sandra Robertson, Coorparoo, Queensland, Australia

Lili Ann Killian Rosenberg, Jacksonville, OR, USA

Diana Maria Rossi, Berkeley, CA, USA

Jude Schlotzhauer, Schlotzhauer Glass Works, Mechanicsville, VA, USA

Wendy Grossman de Segovia, Rosebud Studios, Phoenicia, NY, USA

Ilana Shafir, Ashkelon, Israel

Saskia Siebrand, Mosaika Art and Design, Montreal, Quebec, Canada

Lillian Sizemore, The San Francisco Mosaic Studio Inc., San Francisco, CA, USA

Robert Stout, Twin Dolphin Mosaics, Ravenna, Italy

Boline Strand, San Francisco, CA, USA

Claudia Tedeschi, Ravenna, Italy

Norman Tellis, Dallas, TX, USA

Steve and Zoe Terlizzese, The Creative Union, Clymer, NY, USA

George Trak, Plovdiv, Bulgaria

Laurel True, True Mosaics, Oakland, CA, USA

Susan Tunick, New York, NY, USA

Valentina Venturi, Ravenna, Italy

Norma Vondee, London, UK

Rosalind Wates, Princes Risborough, Buckinghamshire, UK

Judy Wood, Glasswood Studio, Saskatchewan, Canada

Chrissie Woods, Windermere, Cumbria, UK

Cristina Yazpik, Mexico City, Mexico

Isaiah Zagar, Philadelphia, PA, USA

Carolina Zanelli, Gradisca Di Spilimbergo, Italy

Zantium Mosaics, Wirksworth, Derbyshire, UK

Sarah Zirkel, Zirkel Mosaics, Austin, TX, USA

INDEX

Note: References with **bold** page numbers include mosaic photographs and/or their captions.